successful
CHANGE

how to implement
change through
people

DAVID MILLER

A powerful & practical guide to delivering
effective change in your organisation

ISBN: 978-0-9870848-8-0 (Print Book)

ISBN: 978-0-9870848-9-7 (E-book)

Partner Published with BookPOD

www.bookpod.com.au

www.**change**first.com/change

Changefirst Ltd.
Mill House, Borde Hill Lane,
Haywards Heath,
West Sussex RH16 1XR UK
Tel: +44 (0)1444 450 777

For Susan and Elissa

Acknowledgements

While I have written many articles over the years, this is the first book I have written and, who knows, it may be my last. With that in mind, I intend to act like a surprised Oscar winner and thank everyone as profusely as I can. But firstly let me say that I have been involved in this work for over 25 years and have worked with many great people during that time. I am sure that my ideas and work have been heavily influenced by all of you. Like most people, my thinking and work have become something of a mosaic; some of the pieces of the mosaic are original and some pieces I have been given. If I don't recognise your contribution to my mosaic in this book, then please accept my apologies in advance.

I want to thank all my colleagues who have worked with me since I founded Changefirst in 1995. In particular, I want to thank Audra Proctor and Doug Daniel who have been great colleagues for all of this time. Over the years we have built up a tremendous team of people in Changefirst who, I believe, provide great customer service and deliver our workshops and consulting brilliantly. It goes without saying that the words in this book are said on behalf of everyone at Changefirst rather than being my personal work.

Before Changefirst I worked for a number of organisations but American Express was where I stayed the longest. I had a great time there and thought it was a wonderful company. I worked with too many tremendous people to name them individually. But just to say that – while you may not have noticed it – I learned so much from all of you.

Then I would like to thank our clients. We have trained over 10,000 people since 1995 and worked with hundreds of organisations. A lot of what is in this book was learned from you. Every time we facilitate a workshop or meet a client to talk about their change challenges we learn something that turns out to be of value.

Karen McCreadie has been a tremendous support while I have been writing this book. She has been great at being editor, contributor and motivator all rolled into one package.

Lastly, I can't move on without thanking my wife Susan and daughter Elissa. The combination of working globally for over a quarter of a century and founding and running a company like Changefirst has meant that I have been away more than I ever wanted to be. All I can do in retrospect is to thank you both for your love, patience and support during this time.

"This is the kind of book you carry around with you. In a sea of sameness and 'consultant speak' Miller cuts through the theory and presents insightful, business savvy solutions centered on people. His voice is compelling as he draws from a deep reservoir of experience. It is essential reading for anyone confronted by change and in today's business environment that means everyone!"

Craig Dinsell, EVP Human Resources
Oppenheimerfunds Inc

"As a programme manager I would recommend this book as essential reading for managers about to embark on a business transformation programme. David provides really useful insights and practical approaches based upon his many years of experience, to the project challenges that too often over stress managers when trying to cope with the demands generated by complex programmes of work."

Colin Grace, CEO
Praktis Solutions

"Bridging the gap between having a great strategy on paper and converting those plans into business results is one of the biggest challenges facing any organisation. The powerful insights and practical methodology in this book provide the means to successfully bridge this gap."

Tim Van den Bossche, President Asia-Pacific
Agfa Graphics

"An invaluable pragmatic guide to driving meaningful change. The focus on leading managers and executives through the change cycle will make you stop and think."

Gordon Smith, CEO of Card Services
J.P. Morgan Chase & Co

Contents

Introduction

Introduction

This book is written for people who want to implement major change successfully. I believe that well-planned and executed change management can make your organisations, communities and maybe even your personal life more successful.

In this book I will describe what you need to do to make change successful. It's not a self-help book; neither is it a simple formula for success because there is no simple formula for success. In truth, your ability to become a great change agent will come down to practice, learning from mistakes and simply your willingness to try out ideas. In this book I will share the experience and approach that has consistently worked for me so that, hopefully, you can improve change implementation in your own organisation.

As an agent for change in your organisation – whether as an executive, line manager, project manager, work group leader or supervisor – you will no doubt grapple with the issues described in this book. Whether the change you are involved in is the implementation of new software, product development, a change to the way you communicate with your customers or a full-scale redirection of your business model, all change can be difficult to pull off.

So how do you successfully implement change? How do you navigate the booby traps and avoid all those things that can so easily pull the rug from under you? How do you energise the organisation around the change? How do you build leadership support? How do you engage others to make the transition *"stick"*? How do you make it real for the people who have to change? And, most importantly, how do you do all this while also meeting your existing commitments and still finding time to see your family?

There are many different aspects of change that spring to mind when we talk of change – strategic, technical, process and people. This book is dedicated to the latter. It is, after all, people change that causes the most headaches and it is this type of change that you have to be successful in if you stand any chance of altering the other three. This book, therefore, explores what you need to do to successfully facilitate change when people have to adopt new ways of working that are a significant departure from how they are currently working.

Ronald Heifetz of the Kennedy School of Government talks about this sort of change as being adaptive work: work which requires learning and a change in values, beliefs or behaviour. He points out that often the change is only possible when both parties – the organisation and the employees – make appropriate adjustments. Heifetz uses the example of a patient suffering from heart disease to illustrate his point. The only way such patients can be restored to operating capacity is if they take responsibility for their own health by making appropriate life adjustments. No amount of surgical intervention or prescription drugs will miraculously *"fix"* patients unless they make lifestyle changes to ensure they don't relapse.

In the same way, successful organisational change is an adaptive process that requires the coordinated efforts of a wide range of people at all levels of an organisation who are collectively seeking the same positive outcome. All parties must take responsibility for their role in the success of the change, otherwise relapse is not only possible but highly probable.

When it comes to what actually works regarding change there is no shortage of help. I really admire the work of the pioneers of change management like Richard Beckhard, Kurt Lewin, William Bridges, Daryl Conner, Ed Schein, Noel Tichy and John Kotter. Their early work was so helpful for us in understanding how successful change happens in organisations.

However the world of change management is also full of all sorts of prophets, evangelists, mice moving cheese and consulting firms with the latest, greatest panaceas that are going to miraculously fix everything. Everyone has an opinion about what works – including me, otherwise I wouldn't be writing this book. But there is a world of difference between an opinion and a proven set of processes, skills and tools.

Since the mid-1990s Changefirst has been perfecting processes, skills and tools to help people like you in large private and public organisations who want to be able to implement change more effectively. We have taught over 10,000 people in more than 35 countries worldwide how to successfully build change capabilities into their organisations, and the tools we use are contained in this book.

What we have found is that the process of successful change runs a fairly similar course regardless of how big an organisation is or what the change is. By teaching people how to manage that process, you radically increase the odds of change being implemented effectively and of the organisation reaching its change objectives.

As such, this book is written for change agents – people in organisations who have been given significant change initiatives to plan and execute. If that sounds like you then read on.

Often you need to get results in difficult complex environments. The change itself could range from changes in a call centre, factory, business unit or could involve company-wide global changes. You could be working in a private, public or not-for-profit organisation. You could be at any level of the organisation. All you know is that you have to get change delivered and you need help in answering the question *"How do I make this happen?"*

The real challenge that we face regarding change was highlighted to me beautifully one morning as I was listening to an interview on a BBC radio programme. Jane Joyner, Head of the UK's Education Standards Authority, was explaining to the presenter, John Humphreys, how 14 failing schools had all pulled themselves out of *"special measures"*. She went on to say how strong leadership, discipline and school uniforms had helped turn these schools around. But in particular she was making the point that these schools had built *"change action plans"* and had implemented them fully.

John Humphreys sceptically retorted that, *"This all sounds like – if you don't mind me saying so – a statement of the obvious."* You can maybe understand why he responded in this way. It does all feel like common sense. Build a plan and then follow through on it. What could be easier? But as Yogi Berra, legendary US baseball coach, so eloquently pointed out: *"In theory there is no difference between theory and practice, in practice there is."* The problem, as many of us know, is that implementing change successfully is often not that easy – the gulf between theory and practice can be immense. Indeed, if the only competence organisations needed was to be able to *"build good plans"*, market dominance would be won by those who hired the best strategic advisors.

And yet business success is not achieved by those who can build the best strategy, but rather by those who can implement their chosen strategy effectively and sustain it.

Success is about adjusting to the marketplace demands more than having a great strategy. It is about implementing that strategy and, in particular, executing the key changes that are necessary for the organisation to realign itself. It is about the effective translation from theory to practice.

If, however, you look at the independent research data going back thirty years, the omens are not good for most organisations. The majority report that between 60 per cent and 70 per cent of change initiatives fail to deliver what was promised.

In the *2008 IBM Global CEO Study*, CEOs and senior executives from around the world reported that they were being bombarded with change, and many said they were struggling to keep up. In fact, they saw the gap widening between what they had to do and what they were capable of delivering.

Getting change wrong can be very costly. During the 2000s GM and Chrysler have, for a range of reasons, found it difficult to adapt to changing marketplaces and customer expectations – so much so that GM is selling off operations and Chrysler is now owned by Fiat. BMW and Mercedes, on the other hand, did recognise the shifting desires of their consumers and rose to meet those demands. Interestingly, though, even Mercedes made a poor job of integrating Chrysler into its business model. The deal was hard to make, but making it work was the really tough job. Similarly, the *Financial Times* suggested that – prior to the leadership of Jeff Bewkes – Time Warner may have burnt through some £200 billion in shareholder equity with poorly executed acquisitions.

Remember, these are all major organisations, run by smart people. They are corporate giants that have stood the test of time, which begs the question that if these industrial monoliths can get it wrong (and, in some cases, get it fatally wrong) what chance have the rest of us got?

The challenge for organisations is to develop the appropriate strategy and then implement it brilliantly. Looking at the evidence, the more difficult of the two is the implementation. After all, it is not unusual for organisations to develop similar strategies, but one delivers the strategy more successfully than the others. The battle between Coke and Pepsi is an ongoing struggle for supremacy. Over the decades their strategies have often been quite similar but each has dominated at different times. And their respective dominance has, more often than not, come down to leadership and execution. In the 1980s Coke was under the tough leadership of Roberto C. Goizueta, who had fled Castro's Cuba in 1961. He completely overhauled the company with a strategy he called *"intelligent risk taking"*. Brilliantly conceived and executed, this turned Coke into the dominant force in the industry. Following Goizueta's untimely death, that lead was eroded over the next ten years, and finally overturned as Pepsi implemented its own strategy of diversification and acquisition exceptionally well. It was, and always is, the implementation that makes the difference.

Often organisations know what they must do. Senior executives are usually committed to the idea of change. The problem is that they often spend a great deal of time and effort building strategies and developing technical solutions like IT systems, only to see them fail in practice. More often than not, many of these solutions are actually very good. The issue, though, is that executives can spend too much time on creating strategies and looking at solutions – often called the *"What"* – and too little time looking at the *"How"*, the *"How"* being implementation. Some studies show that executives, in less successful changes, can spend something like 90 per cent of their time on the *"What"* versus the *"How"*. And if only 10 per cent of their time is spent working out how the change is going to be implemented effectively, then all you end up with are high-quality solutions with poor-quality implementation. And as a result the business doesn't get the full pay-off from the initiative.

In Chapter One we are going to review some of the statistics around change failures, just so you understand the issues and what you're up against. But ultimately this book is about the most important element of successful change – implementation. It is about your ability to translate a potential solution into day-to-day practical reality. I have seen many initiatives successfully implemented during my career and they always come down to execution. Change can be successful. In fact, in a recent Changefirst survey participants told us that over 50 per cent of their change initiatives were fully operational and doing what they said they would. This compares to 30 per cent success rates in other studies. We'll look at these numbers some more later.

It seems self-evident to us that organisations have to learn how to execute change effectively. Our belief, after working on this for over

20 years, is that consultants can't deliver change for you. They have many skills and capabilities, but it's very hard for external suppliers or partners to be as successful as internal change agents. In a recent Changefirst survey, respondents voted internal teams as being by far the best way to implement change; external consulting firms were one of the least effective. Today we need to develop the capabilities to implement change within our own businesses. If we understand change and, more importantly, have a set of tools, processes and skills to execute change then we can implement change successfully – regardless of what it involves.

Not only does this strengthen the business but it also puts you – the change agent – in a very strong professional position. This book, therefore, offers you a real opportunity to differentiate yourself in your business and future career so that you can consistently demonstrate sought-after change management skills.

Change is therefore without question the biggest strength, weakness, opportunity and threat to your business and your career.

The business and personal case for investing time and effort in developing change management skills is clear:

- You will build a competitive advantage for your organisation by increasing the number of changes that are successfully implemented

- Your organisation will save money. Not only will you benefit from the more successful implementations, but you will also save money by planning and executing change yourself rather than using external consulting support

- You will gain critical personal career skills. As change is the number one constant in organisations, these skills are highly sought after – and once you have learned them you can use them in any environment or situation

Successful change implementation happens when organisations find a way to create real commitment to the new way of working. It happens when people adjust their behaviour to meet the needs of the change and the change is used as intended. And all of that increases the likelihood that the proposed benefits of the change are obtained.

That's what this book is all about. It gives you an overview of our experience and hopefully brings that experience to life through examples, stories and action steps. Please treat the book as an overview of what the Changefirst methodology can deliver for you and your company. It will introduce you to new skills and tools that will increase your personal value and employability now and in the future.

If, after reading this book, you want to know more, go to www.changefirst.com/change and find out about our comprehensive online change tools, e-learning and workshop facilitation services.

PART ONE:

Understanding the change challenge – how organisations and people connect

1

Making the case for change management

There has been a vast amount of research over the last 30 years about the effectiveness of change programmes. Organisations ranging from Gartner Group to Harvard Business School and McKinsey & Company have pointed to the low success rates of major change in organisations. For example, a study of quality initiative implementations in the 1990s pointed to 10 per cent success rates across organisations. Most studies, however, hover around 30 to 40 per cent success rates, depending on the complexity and difficulty of the change attempted.

Those involved in change would, however, probably not be overly surprised. Ask almost any employee in almost any business in almost any part of the world and they will be able to give you stories of change initiatives that went badly wrong or just faded away. They certainly will be able to show you the presentation describing how a certain change was going to radically alter the way things happened, only to become consigned to the *"trash folder"* twelve months later. I, myself, am the proud owner of some novel change memorabilia from the early 1990s. I have, for example, two T-shirts. One says *"We will do it!"* and the second says *"We did it"*. The second was designed to be worn 12 months after launch. Sadly, it is still in its wrapper, awaiting probable sale on eBay. You may well have similar souvenirs and stories that you have experienced or heard about.

But, anecdotes and memorabilia apart, these numbers aren't terribly helpful because we have no idea if those initiatives that *"failed"* used change management techniques or not. We don't know if they differed in their complexity. We don't know the culture of the organisations concerned. We therefore don't actually know anything about the change that can conclusively prove or disprove anything. As a result, I believe that the numbers on *"change failure versus success"* can be misleading. Let me explain why.

For years we ran workshops and talked to executive teams and consulting firms about change implementation. At the time it was fashionable to discuss change in terms of *"success and failure"* and yet we found that senior people often pushed back on this description. Certainly no one wants to admit they have failed, but perhaps there was more to it than that. Invariably, they would talk about relatively high success rates in implementing change. On the ground, the statistics did not match those mentioned by highly reputable organisations such as the Gartner Group. In fact their numbers were often diametrically opposed to those produced by independent researchers. Instead of a 30 per cent success rate, senior teams would sometimes report that more than 70 per cent of their changes were successful. So what was going on? Perhaps it simply wasn't accurate to describe the outcomes in such black and white, clear-cut terms. Certainly we couldn't seem to marry up the two realities.

As we moved down the organisation from the executive team to project teams and middle management, the story started to change slightly as we were given more information. We would hear things like, *"Well, yes it's here and we use it when we have to. But if people can avoid using it, they will"*. And yet clearly the change is there in the business. The new customer system or process is in place; the software and hardware are on site, the technical training has been given and people have been told about it – but there has been no work done to build people's commitment to it or create real behaviour change. Consequently it doesn't really get used. A study by the Gartner Group confirmed that, *"80 per cent of all technology projects were not… used in a way intended or not used at all six months after installation".*

This data is supported by our work and experience. I remember asking a friend of mine about a new Customer Relationship Management (CRM) system that I knew his firm had implemented. He had been with the firm for over 20 years and was one of their best salesmen in the UK. His response was, *"Well, I do anything I can not to use it. I do the bare minimum, otherwise I will have to spend two or three hours on a Saturday getting it right and that's not what I want to be doing. And sometimes it directs me to do something that I know is not going to work, so I ignore it."*

The fact is that change is rarely totally unsuccessful. For example, an IT solution is rarely simply abandoned; more likely, it will be partially used. Perhaps it is used properly by a few employees or for a few specific tasks. Perhaps it is used superficially by people like my friend with the CRM system. But it is rare for someone to simply take the solution away.

It was clear that there were shades of grey that were not being accounted for in the *"success or failure"* viewpoint.

Installing versus implementing change

Describing change in terms of success and failure may be clear-cut and straightforward but it's not accurate. And, perhaps more importantly, it's not helpful. So we began to make a distinction between installation and implementation. This perspective resonated with people up and down the organisation because it was more accurate and more palatable to view change from this standpoint. Senior executives were more likely to say *"Yes, I can see it's been installed"* rather than *"Yes, I can see it failed"*.

Recognising these shades of grey is also essential if you are ever to close the value gap and lift installation into implementation - see Figure 1.1. One of the reasons organisations don't reap the full benefit of change initiatives is that they confuse installation and implementation, and stop at installation. They don't appreciate that installation is just a milestone towards full implementation and, as such, they take their collective foot

Figure 1.1: Implementation versus installation

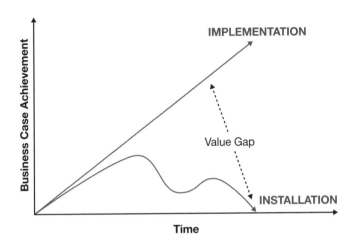

off the accelerator and momentum falls away. Consequently the changes languish at installation, never fully delivering their promised potential. For example, having a new IT system at head office may be successful installation, but if everyone is still using the old system then the change has been a waste of time, money and energy, and has not delivered its rewards.

In a real-life example of how installation can fall short, I was recently working with a well-known business in the UK. Over the years they had acquired numerous companies, some large and some small. On the surface everything appeared integrated: for example, there were shared policies, uniform email addresses and identical branding across the business. On closer inspection it became clear that the employees of many of the acquired companies still saw themselves as part of their original organisation. They acted like people in a rather repressed occupied country. As soon as senior management left the room they reverted to using the name of their old company. They frequently told me how the change process needed to be adapted for the needs of *"their company"* and it also became clear that they still used a set of shadow processes to manage things like customer relationships. They didn't associate or connect to the new business, and all their stories were about how great the old company had been and how inadequate the new one was. Whether the stories were true or down to rose-tinted nostalgia or even sheer bloody-mindedness was irrelevant. What had happened was that there had been no change management process to ensure that people left the past behind and embraced the new organisation in a positive and constructive way.

Change doesn't happen when the new system is in place or the software is uploaded to the servers or the hardware is up and running. It happens when someone engages with the new system and realises that the information they now have access to is better in some way than it would have been with the previous system. It happens when someone says, *"Yes, this system is helpful to me"* or even, *"I've just got to get on with it and learn some new skills"*. In those moments change is implemented, behaviour changes and the full potential of the business case is realised.

The reason the difference between installation and implementation is called a *"value gap"* is because there is a difference between the value that's achieved at installation and the business case or return on investment that was initially predicted. And it is this value gap that is the most powerful case for change management and developing a change capability in every organisation. Without proven change management processes it is very difficult to consistently achieve the organisation's change goals.

You might want to take a moment to think about change in your organisation and take a guess at what the value gap may be. When we run workshops we usually have a good deal of ceiling staring and chin rubbing before someone bravely suggests, *"Oh, I don't know, but it will be a lot!"* Occasionally we have had senior participants make a few high-level estimates, based on the number of previous initiatives and their respective success, and announcing that the company was probably some $80 million out of pocket. We've even had the odd client admit to more than $100 million across their global operation!

You'll never reach 100 per cent implementation in all your initiatives, but there is a huge financial reward and competitive edge to be enjoyed by any organisation that can successfully close that value gap. A recent Changefirst study indicated that on large projects where more than £1 million was spent on implementation, change management can add £6.50 of value for every pound spent. So the potential gains are enormous.

The costs of installed change

There are four main costs associated with settling for installed change:

- Installed change is expensive
- Installed change extracts a high people cost
- Installed change costs leaders their credibility
- Installed change makes your organisation a poor competitor in the marketplace

Installed change is expensive

Whether you are implementing new technology or are radically altering a business process, there is always a financial cost involved. In one study conducted in 2004, John McManus and Trevor Wood-Harper showed that the estimated cost of IT project failure alone across the European Union was a staggering 142 billion Euros. Professor Chris Clegg of the University of Sheffield conducted research into the same area and discovered that as much as £58 billion is wasted in IT-related change in the UK every year. Our guess is that these estimates only include large IT changes; imagine how big that number would be if you included all IT change. Much of the true waste in change is lost through smaller failed initiatives.

I remember talking with a very senior programme director for a FTSE 100 company one day. He told me that in his organisation you could be in charge of a change project worth up to £5 million, and if it was installed and no benefits resulted few questions were asked. Those involved were simply not held accountable for these *"small"* change projects. Apparently the executive team were only interested in the £5-million-plus projects. If any of them *"went south"*, then the people leading those initiatives could find themselves dealing with a whole set of negative outcomes.

I am someone who has worked with and for global companies for nearly 25 years, but even I was surprised. Even assuming that these accounts may have been embellished by a little hubristic exaggeration, the implications are enormous. If what he says is true – and I have no reason to believe otherwise – it's likely that it is also true of many large organisations. In which case the aggregated amount of failed change across all organisations must be colossal.

Not only does this highlight the massive financial cost of poorly implemented change, but it also demonstrates the impact on people.

Installed change extracts a high people cost

If the evidence suggests that a fraction of attempted change is implemented, then the majority of people involved in change will only have experienced installation – at best. This has serious repercussions for employee engagement. The comprehensive data held by the polling organisation Gallup, who research human nature and behaviour in organisations, suggests that in an average organisation, the ratio of engaged to actively disengaged employees is only 1.5 to 1. In other words for every three engaged employees there are two who are actively disengaged!

As a comparison, world-class organisations record an engagement ratio near 8 to 1, meaning there are eight engaged employees for every disengaged one. Within the US workforce, Gallup estimates the cost of disengagement to be more than $300 billion in lost productivity alone.

What is interesting is that one of the major influencing factors in employee engagement is the degree to which all employees see the organisation successfully implementing change. Being part of change initiatives that constantly fail or end up at installation demotivates people and saps their energy, focus and excitement. And it's not good news for those leading the change either.

Installed change costs leaders their credibility

As a change agent or change leader, if you keep announcing changes to your employees and nothing much happens it creates cynicism and lowers trust.

This means leaders pay the highest price for failed or installed change – they lose their credibility. The very core of leadership is trust, and installed initiatives erode that trust at an alarming rate. In our work the most frequent question we get asked is, *"How do I persuade my boss to demonstrate support for this change?"* This becomes even more pressing if that boss has a track record of installation. It creates the *"palm tree effect"*. When the leader announces yet another change, the employees simply adopt the characteristics of a palm tree in a storm. They bend over to accommodate the storm, but once the storm has passed the trees spring right back to their original position as if nothing had happened.

Unfortunately for the leader, the palm tree effect isn't always personal. If the organisation has a legacy of failed or installed change, it can be very hard to break down the resulting cynicism and persuade others that a new leader is going to make the difference. In those situations the palm tree effect will prevail.

Installed change makes you a poor competitor

If it's necessary to stay a step ahead of the competition or regain lost market share, then installation will have obvious repercussions for your competitive advantage. It is clear that the organisations which will prosper are the ones who can effectively implement change, adapt to changing consumer trends and so on, regardless of their market position or dominance. Many competitors have very similar strategies but it's their respective ability to execute those strategies that sets them apart.

There is also an opportunity cost associated with installed change. We all have a finite amount of time in our working day. If you or your employees or colleagues are preoccupied with change, especially change that doesn't end up meeting the expected business objectives, then the business has without doubt lost valuable working hours that can never be recovered. Those working hours could have been put to better, more profitable, use elsewhere. In fact, in some cases it has been found that shareholders or taxpayers would have been better off if the organisation had simply given them the budget spent on the change initiative.

Successful implementation is not free

Clearly implementing change, rather than just installing it, brings enormous benefits – but there are costs associated with implementation too. Let's run through the organisational costs associated with implementing change.

You have to appoint a dedicated resource to lead the change management activities. Depending on the size of the project this could be one person or a group. In our experience, asking part-time project team members to take responsibility for a major change project is a significant risk factor in change.

You have to allow more time for all the change management activities to roll out. Well-planned and executed involvement, learning and communications do take more time to deliver. The goal is to create momentum early in the project by engaging with people. Out of this you want to create a *"snowball"* effect – where you pick up speed as the project gains traction over time.

You have to train your people to be effective in planning and executing change. This takes time and money. You can get change management from untrained project team members; it's just not likely to be very good change management. You need to train people to be able to plan, execute and track change activities, especially those activities that involve and impact on other people. You need your people to have skills in areas such as communication, behavioural change and involvement.

Nothing worth having in life is free and sustainable change is no exception. Implementation can be costly but is nowhere near as costly as failed or installed and failed change. The rewards of seeing a change initiative through installation to ownership and engagement are exponentially increased if you use change management to drive towards implementation.

2

Change happens one person at a time – the personal dynamics of change

When J.P. Garnier, the former CEO and Chairman of pharmaceutical company GlaxoSmithKline (GSK), was interviewed about executing change, he said, *"Getting people to change – one by one – is the only way to change organisations. After all, every change is personal"*.

Garnier did a great job in describing the core issue in organisational change. In business, where complexity is often admired over simplicity, it can be tempting to think about big concepts – like change programmes, roll outs, re-engineering, outsourcing – as being the crux of successful change. As such, it is all too easy to forget the reality: that it is the people involved in the change who need to adapt and evolve to make that change successful.

Change is no longer a one-off isolated event. Individuals within organisations are being asked to deal with multiple changes that reach into all aspects of their lives. New IT systems, new customer service processes, new organisational structures, new management, new finance procedures – you name it, someone is going to change it. And this doesn't include the changes people have to deal with in their personal lives. The aggregate result for many people is an overwhelming amount of change.

There is so much more change than there ever used to be. And it's not just the speed and amount of change that's making a difference. Advancing technology renders innovations obsolete very quickly; readily accessible information means the customer is more discerning and demands better service, higher quality and reasonable prices. For many businesses competition is no longer limited to geographical location.

On top of all that, society is changing. Twenty-five years ago a *"job for life"* was normal. Thirty years of service and a gold watch were commonplace. Today the average person will change jobs several times and is even likely to change careers, locations and/or employment status during their working life. The way you interact with society and how you consume has also changed and will almost certainly continue to do so.

In the late 1990s we were reassured by various *"gurus"* and motivational speakers that we shouldn't worry too much about the increasing amount of change because human beings were built for change. In fact, we should learn to love it through the *"simple"* step of changing our mindset. The problem is that most of us don't love change – especially the disruptive, uncontrollable variety.

We're all control freaks

The truth is, we don't really like major change very much at all. Most people prefer the status quo or changing slowly at their own pace. Human beings have been evolving for millions of years. The new field of scientific research known as evolutionary psychology holds that while we inhabit a thoroughly modern world of technological innovation, exploration and almost constant change we do so with the ingrained mentality of our Stone Age ancestors. In other words, we may have taken the man out of the Stone Age, but we have not taken the Stone Age out of the man.

So while our basic human hardwiring hasn't changed much, our need to deal with change has – even over two or three generations. And that has repercussions.

Our work demonstrates what social science has long believed to be true – people have a very strong control orientation. We are innately driven to seek and find control over our lives. We gain a sense of comfort and well-being from the certainty we perceive and when those perceptions are rocked, we are rocked. Think of change as disrupting our perception of control. Change often makes us feel as though we are losing control and that sensation makes us instinctively resist whatever we perceive is happening to us.

We are therefore often not reacting to the change itself but to what that change brings and the impact it may have on us. We may want to move house, for example, but the disruption that comes with that move causes us to delay action. The idea of having to spend countless Saturday mornings looking at possible houses, dealing with lawyers, getting the funding approved from the bank, finding new schools for the kids, working out a new commute to the office, joining new clubs and then packing and unpacking can be overwhelming.

The control issue is vitally important to change agents. You should never under-estimate its importance. In his book *59 Seconds* Professor Richard Wiseman quotes the work of Ellen Langer at Harvard University:

"Half of the residents in a nursing home were given a houseplant and asked to look after it while the other half were given an identical plant but told that the staff would take responsibility for it. Six months later, the residents who had been robbed of even this small amount of control over their lives were significantly less happy, healthy and active than the others. Even more distressingly, 30 per cent of residents who had not looked after their plant had died, compared to 15 per cent of those who had been allowed to exercise such control. The message is clear – those who do not feel in control of their lives are less successful, and less psychologically and physically healthy, than those who do feel in control."

Don't surprise people!

Once you see change through the lens of control you can begin to appreciate what happens to people when you announce changes. This is particularly true when you announce changes that they weren't expecting.

Change disrupts the strong conscious or unconscious feelings of control that people develop in the status quo or current state. Consequently people in the midst of change often feel uncertain and fearful. They are worried that they may lack the capacity to change; they may have so many other changes going on that they simply don't have the capacity to cope with more. They may also be worried about not having the necessary skills. The idea of learning a new way of operating can cause discomfort, as people are often unsure if they still possess the competencies they will need to pull it off. In addition, they may lack the confidence that they will be able to operate in the new way. People usually build up a certain level of confidence in the way they work now; it can shake their confidence if they have to unlearn all of that and operate in a new way. And they will be uncomfortable with new ways of working and new working relationships; there is a level of comfort in being able to do your job well enough not to cause any stress. Plus, when tasks and responsibilities change, working relationships can be altered; people often lose established relationships and worry about how new ones will work.

Unfreeze – change – freeze

In the 1940s, psychologist Kurt Lewin explained that there were three basic stages to the personal change process, and his theory has formed the basis of our understanding of how people adapt to change ever since. Lewin's model shows how people move through three distinct stages:

1. Unfreezing
2. Change
3. Freezing

The first part is, as the name would suggest, an unfreezing or thawing of the old way. People in the organisation are made aware of the need for change. They are being asked to effectively unlearn old ways. Here natural defence mechanisms have to be bypassed and people need to be reassured about the validity and necessity of the change.

The second stage is the actual change, where people experiment with the new ways of working or behaving. This is typically a confusing time of transition. Those in this stage know something is different and they are heading somewhere new, but are as yet unclear what that final destination will actually be like.

The third and final stage is the refreezing, where people employ new skills and attitudes and are rewarded by the organisation. Here the new way becomes the norm and a level of comfort returns to the individuals involved.

"Freezing" implies the end of the process as the change is solidified into daily practice, but this is not what Lewin intended. He saw the three stages as a continuous process of unfreezing, changing and freezing, during which one set of changes is constantly followed by another set of changes.

Turbulent transitions

How deep or how difficult the transition from current state to future state is depends on the change and the individuals involved in that change, plus the amount and complexity of change they are being expected to handle.

In her book *On Death and Dying*, Swiss-born psychiatrist Elisabeth Kübler-Ross described the *"five stages of grief"* model. These are the stages that people go through when diagnosed with a terminal illness and facing death. Her five stages are denial, anger, bargaining, depression and acceptance.

This insightful model was later built upon and developed by industrial psychologists who recognised the correlation between the grief stages and the processes people go through when confronted with change. Subsequent models added additional stages to make it easier to use in an organisational setting.

- **Shock:** *"I didn't see that coming."*
- **Denial:** *"Oh, look, it won't affect me anyway." "If I keep my head down it will blow over and we can get back to normal."*
- **Anger:** *"Not another change initiative." "Why can't they just leave it alone; it's never going to work, anyway!" "They have no idea what goes on at the moment and now they want to change it." "I don't have time."*

Figure 2.1: Reactions to change

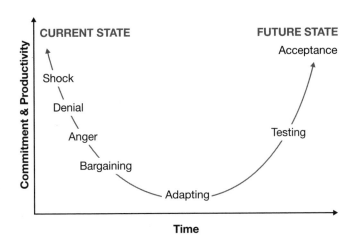

- **Bargaining:** *"If I take on that extra task you wanted me to do, can I be exempt from the change?"*
- **Adapting:** *"This doesn't look like it's going away, so I am going to have to make some changes." "I'll just make some little changes and that will make it easier."*
- **Testing:** *"Well, this is actually easier than the old way now I've got the hang of it." "It does save me time and it's not that hard to use, so maybe I'll give it a go."*
- **Acceptance:** *"OK, I can see the benefits of the change. It was worth the investment and it's made my life easier." "I can get access to the information I need much faster with this change and that's helped me do my job better."*

How smooth this path is depends on how big the change is and how much resistance you meet on the journey. As we've discovered, human beings aren't that crazy about change. We like to know where we are in the world; we like to know what we are doing and to feel confident that we can do what is asked of us. When that certainty is challenged we will instinctively resist it.

Resistance is natural

Resistance is the behavioural consequence when someone feels that they have lost control of a situation. If someone believes that they are losing control they will instinctively *"slam on the brakes"*, and once this has happened it can be extremely difficult to create any acceleration.

If someone feels that their level of understanding or comfort is being threatened and they are not sure what will happen to them, they start resisting. And, generally speaking, the greater the level of disruption to them the higher the level of resistance that results. It's important to understand that resistance is a natural part of the process. You should educate your managers so that they navigate it rather than waste time and energy trying to eradicate it. A key indicator of success will be your managers' ability to help people to adapt to change.

I was running a workshop a few years ago and a sales manager told me that her people had simply gone through too much change: *"They just aren't interested any more. Many of them are looking for jobs in other companies – where 'the grass is greener' – and others are at work but not really present."* Daryl Conner, author of *Managing at the Speed of Change*, describes this state as being like a bath sponge that's already full of water. No matter how much more water you pour onto the sponge, no more will be assimilated.

Most of us have a fairly fixed capacity for change. We may differ in our capacity to accept and assimilate change. But we all have a ceiling. In other words, we all have a limit to the amount of change we can handle at any given time. This limit is made up of both personal changes and work-driven changes.

If individuals have a finite capacity for change and organisations are simply collections of individuals, then it's safe to assume that organisations also have a finite capacity for change. Organisations are, after all, the aggregate of the people who work there.

The main cause of this problem, in our experience, is what is sometimes called *"perpetual loading"*. Organisations keep constantly piling on one change after another. These changes are often complex, overlapping and come quickly one after the other. Employees become worn down by the continuous change. This is compounded by the lack of respite, so employees have little opportunity to recover their capacity. A recent survey published in the Harvard Business Review reported that 86 per cent of employees complained that their firms didn't allow enough time for reflection and regeneration after stressful phases (of change). With little time to recover and poor line of sight to the end of the turmoil, employees become unengaged and dispirited. More than anything they are suffering from *"change fatigue"*. One of our observations, incidentally, is that you see this fatigue in executives as well as front-line workers.

This book is about implementing single changes and is not focused on curing the problem of perpetual loading. But if organisations want to be more successful in implementing change, clearly they need to try and end this cycle of continuous and unremitting change.

Change often has positive outcomes for people

It's very easy, when we talk about change, control and resistance, to see change as an experience that has no positive results. It's all just uncomfortable and disruptive. But we learn and adapt through change. Like many people, when I look back on my life it's often been the most difficult changes which have taught and helped me the most.

Mihaly Csikszentmihalyi, the Hungarian psychology professor at the Drucker School of Management at Claremont Graduate University in California, writes in his classic book *Flow*:

"Contrary to what we usually believe, the best moments in our lives, are not the passive, receptive, relaxing times – although such experiences can also be enjoyable, if we have worked hard to attain them. The best moments usually occur when a person's body or mind are stretched to their limits in a voluntary effort to accomplish something difficult and

worthwhile... Such experiences are not necessarily pleasant at the time they occur... Getting control of life is never easy, and sometimes if can be definitely painful. But in the long run optimal experience adds up to a sense of mastery – or perhaps better, a sense of participation in determining the content of life – that comes as close to what is usually meant by happiness as anything else we can conceivably imagine."

Change can be an exciting time of learning and reinvention. Resilient people grasp that opportunity and use the experience to propel them forward.

Change really does happen *"one person at a time"*. It's easy, even convenient, to forget about the people – but if you want beneficial implemented change instead of expensive failed or installed change then you simply can't. My observation, over the years, is that very often the difference between installed and implemented change is down to the leader's willingness to embrace this simple reality. People are always the key to successful change. Very often, you can achieve installation with brute force and ignorance but it takes coordination and cooperation to achieve ownership where the change delivers all its promise. Very often, leaders who are not good at achieving implementation find ways to ignore this advice. You'll hear them say things like *"Our people are very bright so they will just get it"*, *"They will have to do it, no choice"* or *"This is just an IT change."* My advice to you is to be very careful about proceeding with change if leaders have this mindset. Help them understand how the change is going to impact on people and how they are likely to react to the change before you move forward.

3. Culture is everything

It's impossible to talk about change without discussing culture. So let's discuss it briefly here.

Lou Gerstner, the former CEO of IBM, said in his memoirs – *Who says Elephants can't Dance? Inside IBM's Historic Turnaround* – "*The thing I have learned at IBM is that culture is everything.*"

What he meant was that it is easy to think about culture as being another dimension to the business like systems or strategy but, in fact, culture influences everything a business does. The way you build your strategy is influenced by your culture. How you manage your customers is directly correlated with your culture. A recent McKinsey survey indicated that the capabilities we build in organisations are more likely to be connected to our culture rather than any analysis of what the business actually needs to be doing in order to be successful. In other words, it is culture that dictates what we do rather than necessity or strategy. Nothing is left untouched by culture. Gerstner's point was that in order to transform IBM he had to come to grips with that fact.

And he is not alone. For many change agents, culture creates something of a dilemma. On the one hand, you can't ignore it; on the other, it's incredibly difficult to change it.

When I first started helping to implement change I would treat every change initiative as being a culture change effort. (Looking back, I think that if senior management had asked me to redesign the staff restaurant I would have described it as a cultural change project!). However, describing change in terms of culture would often make change plans more complex than they needed to be. It certainly extended the time needed to implement the change and, frankly, it would unnecessarily *"frighten the horses"*. Often senior leaders would suddenly see the change as being too daunting to lead and would start resisting the change themselves. Having said that, there are clearly some initiatives that are really big culture change shifts and need all the heavyweight change tools that you can bring to bear to offer any chance of success.

What I eventually found helpful was to think about culture change in two different ways. They are both about changing people's behaviours and values but they are very different in their focus, impact and success rates.

The first type of cultural change is the type Gerstner talks about in his book. This involves changing the culture of the organisation in a very fundamental way. In IBM's case there were multiple strands to the change. For example, IBM moved to being more rooted in a service culture, it rebuilt a climate of real accountability and it moved to a more relaxed culture in line with the types of organisations found in Silicon Valley. This type of culture change is very difficult. In fact, some studies – such as the Business Intelligence report *Managing and Sustaining Radical Change* – have indicated that there is a less than one in ten chance that you will be successful. Certainly what I have observed over 25 years is that these changes require enormous leadership and organisational effort to pull them off.

A colleague of mine – who is a well known consultant in the field of culture change – told me of the time he visited the head office of a large retail organisation in the UK for an introductory meeting. The company HR executives spent a lot of time emphasising how important it was to achieve this change for the future of the enterprise. When my friend began to spell out what it might take to pull it off they were appalled and told him, *"You don't understand, we can't afford to make people unhappy. We need a light touch here!"* When he suggested that these two goals were incompatible they told him they would look for a more skilled and sympathetic consultant. Wise man that he is, my colleague left without objection and never contacted the company again. The thing these executives did not know – and my colleague and Gerstner did – was that a *"light touch"* rarely changes culture. It's tough work and this book is therefore not really concerned with this type of change. For an introduction to the subject, Lou Gerstner's book is very readable and *Good to Great* by Jim Collins is a different, more analytical take on the subject.

The second type of cultural change comes about through the adoption of behaviours which are needed for specific changes to be successful. A very basic example would be that when you implement new technology you sometimes need people to change certain behaviours such as being more accurate, more timely or letting the system dictate when certain customers should be called. This behaviour-led approach is the focus of this chapter. I see little evidence that this type of change is anywhere near as difficult to pull off as the organisation-wide cultural change such as the change Gerstner had to grapple with.

So the answer to the dilemma is simple. Don't ignore culture, just focus on changing behaviour so that the change is successfully implemented, the culture is neutralised and shifts naturally over time.

Defining culture

There are many definitions of organisational culture. The one we find most useful is that culture is *"the sum of a group's behaviour, way of working, ideas, beliefs and values"*.

Other explanations talk about *"the way we work around here"* or *"the total sum of the values, customs, traditions and meanings that make a company unique"*. I am not sure the exact definition is terribly important as long as we are talking about the same thing and that we understand the often intangible elements that come together to create a culture.

An organisation grows over time and eventually reaches maturity. This was described by Andy Grove in his excellent book *Only the Paranoid Survive*. He called the maturity phase *"harvesting"*.

Basically, by the time the business reaches the *"harvest phase"* it has established well-defined rules and norms which have developed to govern the way the business operates. This usually works well until market conditions change and those well-established rules and norms start causing operational or strategic problems; we saw this with Hewlett Packard in the 1990s and GM in the 2000s. This is a time when we often keep using existing ways to try and solve new problems, leading to frustration and decline - as shown in Figure 3.1. Grove describes the point when you have the possibility of adopting new ways of working as the *"inflection point"*.

In order to shift your culture you first have to understand it, and that's the challenge. If you have been in the company as it has grown and developed it is often difficult, maybe almost impossible, for you to understand your own organisational culture. You are an integral part of that culture and as such you automatically take many of the rules and processes that govern the way you operate for granted.

What three monkeys told us about culture

There is a supposedly true story about the results of some research into animal behaviour that I think perfectly illustrates the primary challenge we face with cultural change.

There are three monkeys in an enclosure, and above the third monkey there is a pole with a bunch of bananas at the top. The third monkey naturally reaches for the bananas, and as he takes one the other two monkeys are soaked with high-power water hoses. It doesn't hurt the monkeys but it's an unpleasant experience for them.

Needless to say, the two wet monkeys are unhappy with the turn of events and glare at the third monkey who is busily munching on his favourite food. None of the monkeys realise there is a connection between the soaking and the bananas – yet. As monkey number three tries to climb the pole and reach for another banana, the other two are soaked again. By the time the third monkey has eaten half a dozen bananas, the other two are very upset. So much so, that as soon as the third monkey reaches for yet another banana the other two attack to stop him eating the bananas. They have developed what Ivan Pavlov calls a conditioned response. Remember, Pavlov was the scientist who conditioned his dogs to salivate to the sound of a bell simply by feeding the dogs and ringing the bell at the same time.

Monkeys one and two have connected *"getting wet"* to *"bananas"*. This is all quite straightforward until the scientist replaces the third monkey with a new monkey. The new monkey spots the bananas and as he stretches out his arm, he is immediately attacked by the other two monkeys. The new monkey doesn't quite understand why, but quickly stops going after the bananas. Some time passes and the scientists replace one of the *"wet"* monkeys with a new monkey. This new monkey again goes for the bananas and the other two attack him. Then the scientist replaces the third original monkey with a new one. This new monkey goes for the bananas and is

Figure 3.1: Organisational renewal

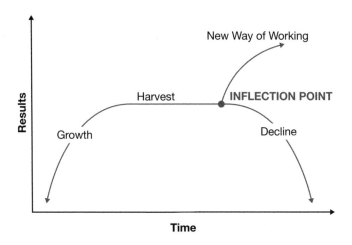

immediately attacked, and has no idea why – but stops trying to get the bananas. Even when all the monkeys are replaced, and therefore none of them have actually experienced the reward and punishment system, no new monkey even attempts to eat the bananas. The reward/punishment system created a way of operating within the enclosure that all new monkeys adopted as the cultural norm and accepted. To them, it was *"just what happens around here"* even though they had no idea why. And that's exactly what happens in an organisation. Let me try and put some framework around this and then move to what you can reasonably do about it.

Organisational culture is made up of the three elements shown in Figure 3.2.

- **Behaviour:** you can see, hear and touch behaviour – it's tangible and can be measured.
- **Known rules:** these are usually written down or at least exist in someone's head and, as such, are easy to discover. They will usually drive behaviour and that isn't necessarily a problem.
- **Hidden rules:** these are never written down; more often than not, they are unconscious. They are understood through experience and taken for granted by those in the organisation. Hidden rules are to people what water is to fish. A fish has no awareness of the water it swims in; people who have been indoctrinated into an organisational culture have no awareness of the hidden rules they navigate every day. They in turn influence these hidden rules so they gradually evolve over time.

More than anything, the monkey story is about hidden rules. Most of us will have felt like one of those monkeys at some point in our working lives. We join an organisation and we can't work out why something is happening. A colleague of mine, Tony, joined a major UK bank in the 1980s in an executive position. He would attend meetings with a notebook so he could make notes and jot down ideas, just as many of us would. He soon noticed, however, that he was the only person doing this. To make matters worse, it was clear that some of his new colleagues

Figure 3.2: Components of organisational culture

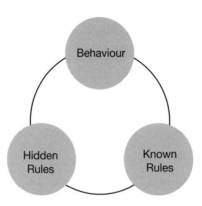

were visibly sneering at him when he made notes in his book. Eventually, after a few weeks, Tony asked what was happening and was told, *"Our executives are too senior to need to make their own notes"*. Tony had inadvertently uncovered a hidden rule about seniority and status in the bank. He left a few months later to go to a job where he was a closer fit to the organisation's culture.

These rules are not written down; you won't read them in the company policy and procedure documentation. They probably won't even be articulated until, like Tony, you ask a direct question. If you are curious about what the hidden rules are in your organisation, try interviewing a new member of staff in the first few weeks of work. If they are open about what they perceive you may discover the *"rules"* of your organisation. Usually when someone new starts they will see the business through new eyes, and for a brief window in time you may get some insight into the hidden rules that govern the business.

Cultural change has a greater capacity than other change initiatives for going wrong because of these hidden rules. Culture affects everything from how change is initiated within a business to how it's managed and what the legacy of change has been. Cultural influences seep into all aspects of an organisation and yet culture is in many ways intangible.

There are two main schools of thought when it comes to culture change. One is the behaviourist view which states that in most situations if you shift the behaviour and get people to start doing something different most adults will tend to keep doing it. This works most of the time. The only time it won't work is when you are trying to impose change that directly conflicts with some deeply held values. For example, quite rightly, you may struggle to get devout Christians to work on a Sunday or Orthodox Jews to work on a Saturday.

The other school of thought says that you can only change culture by actually changing the *"hidden rules"* because they are so powerful. This is probably true when you are asking the people in the organisation to make very deep changes in the way they value things or feel about them. The problem is that it can take years to achieve – and, most importantly, success rates when using this approach can be very low.

Our major focus at Changefirst is therefore to provide change agents with tools and processes to help change people's behaviour so it matches the requirements of the change in line with the second and much more successful type of cultural change we talked about earlier.

Focus on behaviour

From a practical perspective, most business people who are interested in change will end up as *"behaviourists"* even though they understand the hole in the argument. That hole is significant, in that we know that there will be some behaviours that are so deeply influenced by hidden rules and cultural norms that unless we do something about the hidden rules the change won't stick. But, in the absence of any really viable alternative, helping people to change their behaviour is the best and perhaps the only sensible approach for several reasons.

It is generally a better use of your time, for a start. Focusing on behaviour allows you to scope out the project in terms of what needs to be changed and to concentrate on finding out what behavioural changes will cement the change. Then changing people's behaviour is an effective way to change organisational culture. Supporting people to learn new behaviours and unlearn old ones can be extremely powerful. And behaviour is the most easily identified, measured and managed of the three cultural components. The ability to measure is an essential part of successful culture change and behaviour is really the only part of culture you can accurately measure.

People mostly learn and change by doing. People need to discuss the change first but change leaders should encourage people to test things out, learn new skills and use the new behaviours in their daily work. That is what beds the change down into the organisation. Adults seem to like doing something and learning from the doing rather than spending too long discussing and analysing.

Even though the focus is on behaviour, it's important to try to understand what the current hidden rules are. There are two key questions here. The first is whether the hidden rules will impede or stop the new behaviours being adopted – are the changes you need to make very deep and significantly impacted by the hidden rules of your organisation? The second is how strong the change implementation actions will need to be. For example, is there a strong relationship between how deeply the current culture is embedded and the need for positive, active involvement by change agents? In other words, the deeper and more entrenched the culture, the stronger the leadership action must be.

As a change agent, if your change is dependent on a deep-seated, well-established culture changing in a fundamental way then think about how you could *"change the change"*. If you can, try to get the strategy or solution to fit the existing culture rather than attempting to change the culture to fit the strategy or solution. This approach can still deliver your objectives and will exponentially increase the possibilities of success.

Six actions to change behaviour

We have collated a set of researched guidelines to help people to change the behavioural elements of projects and initiatives:

1. Keep the behaviour change components as manageable as you can. Tactics to achieve this include phasing the change effort across businesses or business units rather than a *"big bang"* blanket approach; cascading the change down the management hierarchy one step at a time; creating bite-sized changes that are easier for people to digest and implement; and restricting the change to smaller units first so you can see the effects *"on the ground"*, which allows you to make adjustments prior to roll out for maximum impact.

2. Ensure executives take a very active role and lead by example.

3. Encourage middle and front-line managers to own the change as quickly as possible.

4. Address the personal needs of people. If you want behaviour change then you need to help people adapt.

5. Focus on the future. It is important to understand and acknowledge where people are now, but spend most of the time helping people to move to the new way of working.

6. Ensure the change is driven by an important business initiative – for example, improving sales performance. Only embark on vital change initiatives.

Organisational culture is a huge topic and the subject of thousands of books. What really matters, however, is that you have an appreciation for the challenges inherent in change initiatives that bump up against corporate culture and for how to manage those situations effectively. Don't worry too much about the hidden rules that are simmering under the surface; instead just focus on the behaviour you need people in the organisation to exhibit. In the next chapter we will explore exactly how to do that as we review the six critical success factors that need to be in place in order to change people's behaviour effectively and sustainably.

4

Six critical success factors for implementing change

For over 15 years we have been helping people like you to implement change that *"sticks"* using a people-focused approach. We call it People-Centred Implementation (or PCI). As the name would suggest, PCI revolves around the people involved in change and teaching those in key positions how to develop change capabilities now and in the future. By transferring PCI techniques and skills to over 10,000 people in 35 countries we have successfully armed those change agents with vital change skills. This, in turn, has allowed them to teach those same skills to others and to disseminate change management capabilities to other people in their organisations.

PCI allows you to build commitment in your people and deal with the inevitable resistance that change brings. Successful change is not characterised by the absence of resistance; resistance is unavoidable in major change. It's a challenge, but with the right tools it is a natural phenomenon to be navigated rather than a road block to halt progress. This book will teach you how you can change behaviour and create ownership in your organisation so that successful change becomes the norm and not the exception.

In order to be a successful change agent you need a comprehensive set of skills, processes and tools at your disposal. Often the problem is that change agents can find one process or tool that works and then use it repeatedly. That may work some of the time but it's often inadequate for getting the job done. It's rather like being a mechanic who only owns a screwdriver – you can work on certain parts of the engine but you can never get the bolts off. In the same way change agents who rely too heavily on a limited set of tools, processes and skills can only work effectively on some change issues. For example, you may believe that the key to successful change lies in being able to identify and work effectively with influential people within the organisation. Certainly this can be very important, but influence alone will never fully compensate for a poor engagement plan. Taking in isolation certain tools and processes will only ever get you so far. What you need is a comprehensive approach that works all the time, regardless of the size or breadth or depth of the change.

Organisational and local change

Change management is often defined as a set of structures, processes, tools and skills which plan and execute change within a certain timeframe, and a set of techniques that help individuals and teams adapt to change. It is the combination of these two components that makes change successful.

Successful change implementation is about creating synergy and connectivity between the organisational transition process and the individual's personal change process. In other words, you need to match what the company needs with what the people in the company can potentially accomplish. Change can be strategised in the executive team boardroom – but unless someone or a team of people cascade that change strategy out to the organisation and its divisions, it will make no difference to people in a factory or in a country or in a plant somewhere. And if it makes no difference to them, then it makes no difference to the organisation or its balance sheet.

To ensure the change is implemented and not just pontificated, it needs to occur at the organisational level as well as the local level. That's why you need front-line employees and middle managers to drive the change in the local operation. If this is not done the change will not happen. Bosses in some far-off location may tell employees to change, but unless there are people on the ground building commitment and driving that change through, the individuals involved in the change will merely direct their considerable creativity towards ways to ignore or thwart it.

The organisational success factors are often a set of actions taken at the global, programme or project level of a change initiative. And yet it's the structured work that is done by senior change agents that creates acceptance of the change. If this is done well it is, in our experience, the work of the change agent to – for example – build a communication plan or create a scoping document that effectively translates the organisational success factors into local behaviour changes.

The local success factors are a set of actions that give the project real traction. This is where change management is tailored and adapted for local groups and involves people having to actually change their behaviour. The local group might be in a country, factory or call centre - as in Figure 4.1. By its very nature it is less structured and more personal.

Figure 4.1: Components of organisational change

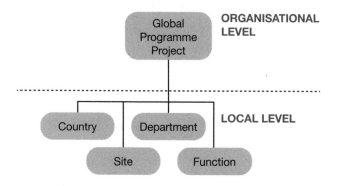

For example, it may involve front-line managers coaching people through change or role modelling the changes in behaviour that are needed. Our experience shows that this work, when done well, moves people from potential resistance to the change to acceptance and eventually commitment. It would appear in many cases that commitment is only possible if change is personalised.

The synergy or balance between organisational and local is important. If the organisational change effort exceeds the local change effort then you may simply create compliance. If there is considerable effort and pressure being exerted from the top down, those doing the work and involved In the change may not be able to ignore it forever but will very often feel resentful at the lack of consultation – and the very best you can hope for is compliance. Compliance is never as potent as committed implementation.

If, on the other hand, the emphasis is the other way around and the local change effort exceeds the organisational change effort, you could have an inconsistently implemented change initiative. Only when change is driven from an organisational level with full commitment do you have a level of strategic and tactical guidance about how the change will operate on the ground. If that detail is not there at the start then individuals on the ground will fill in the blanks themselves, and it's therefore highly likely that each local operation will create a slightly different interpretation of the change. The result is that you will have slightly different initiatives at each local operation and the change will therefore not be consistent across the operation as a whole.

A global technology organisation we worked with had this very problem. They needed to implement a new CRM (Customer Relationship Management) system. The shareholder logic was impeccable. They suffered from all sorts of issues with account management brought on by the fact that many of their customers were global. Getting the people in Canada to understand what was happening to their customers in Europe was vital. Sizeable revenue opportunities were being missed.

Clearly this was a challenge. They had a strong organisational imperative to fix the challenge, so they launched the new system with a flurry of executive announcements, web-based communication sessions, technical training, etc. The problem was that locally their sales people had a very different perspective. They never understood why this was important to them personally. What the company saw as a key imperative, they saw as increased bureaucracy and time spent away from customers. The organisation had to rewind the initiative and spend a lot of time working face-to-face with the sales force to revitalise the change. There was no consideration for the local implications of the change, and consequently the company lost eighteen months and millions of dollars. Subsequently a real focus on the local issues turned the change around and eventually the system began to function as intended.

Organisation and local change need to mesh. We are now going to look at the six critical success factors to ensure they do. Three are organisational success factors and three are local success factors, and together they facilitate the delivery of effective change.

The critical success factors

Here is a quick overview of the six critical success factors (CSFs). The rest of the book will cover these in more detail and show you how to put them into operation. It's important to remember that each of these factors describes a desired outcome. So, for example, CSF 1: Shared Change Purpose is what should be happening in the organisation if you are successful. Everyone will know about the purpose of the change because you will have shared it successfully.

CSF1: Shared Change Purpose

You want to create and share a powerful case for change in the organisation. Your hope is that this achieves more than awareness and that it creates some energy and buzz but, at a minimum, you must achieve clarity – certainly in the people who will need to adapt to the changes. You want people to understand why the change is needed.

Figure 4.2: The Changefirst "Wheel": Six critical success factors

CSF 2: Effective Change Leadership

You want change leaders to provide direction, guidance and support for the change. They need to provide this to the people adapting to and implementing the change. Done well, this allows people to see their leaders demonstrating their own commitment to the change through their actions as well as their words.

CSF 3: Powerful Engagement Processes

You need powerful engagement processes to be put in place which actively engage the organisation in the change process. These engagement processes are designed to foster commitment, encourage new behaviour and teach new skills. Done well, they offer a framework that builds commitment and helps people to undertake the actions they need to do to make the change successful.

CSF 4: Committed Local Sponsors

You need to enable middle and front-line managers to take responsibility for the change in their area of authority. Firstly, they need to commit to the change themselves and demonstrate that commitment. Then they need to lead their change. Done well, this will connect the need for organisational change to the reality of what that means to the people having to change.

CSF 5: Strong Personal Connection

You need to help people to develop a strong personal connection as this builds personal commitment to the change. This can be done, for example, by helping people see how they can be more successful when working in new ways. Done well, this helps people commit to the change sooner and adapt their behaviour more quickly.

CSF 6: Sustained Personal Performance

This is the point at which people's concerns and reactions to the change challenge are effectively addressed. You need to ensure that those involved with the change are helped and supported through the transition process and that their behaviour adapts. Done well, this ensures that people move through the transition stage swiftly so that performance is not adversely affected and/or is maintained during the change process.

Although this is a six-stage model, it is not necessarily sequential. It doesn't have to be implemented *"one through six"*, although that is the most common way to describe the stages. For example, as a change agent you may decide that you need to get more leaders on board or establish if there is any senior support for the change (CSF2) prior to creating a shared change purpose (CSF1). For instance, when I was a corporate change agent I would test the early support for any change by informally locating influential managers in the organisation and gauging their support for the proposed initiative. If support was low, I would consider slowing the process of change until that support could be gathered or I would find ways to get key people to help me craft a different solution. In situations such as this there is no point creating a shared vision if there is no support for it. It would be a waste of time and resources. Once you become more familiar with the model you will be able to decide the most appropriate starting point for your change.

PART TWO:

Organisational success factors – building successful change plans

5

Shared change purpose – making the case for change

In 1969 one of the most complex change projects ever attempted was completed successfully with the words, *"Houston, Tranquillity Base here. The Eagle has landed"*. Later, as he put his left foot down on the moon's surface, Neil Armstrong declared, *"That's one small step for man, one giant leap for mankind."*

It was, of course, the first moon landing. The project had started in the mid-1950s and culminated in success in 1969. In 1962 John F. Kennedy, during a speech in Houston, Texas, announced that, *"America would put a man on the moon by the end of the decade"*. This was a powerful and compelling vision for a change project. One of the major contributing factors for this bold project was the launch by the Russians of Sputnik 1 in 1957, followed by the new R-7 Semyorka rocket with a ballistic missile-carrying capability. These events came as a shock to the Americans, and to NASA in particular. If the Soviets were left unchecked, their early domination of space had potentially significant implications – giving them the possibility of some measure of political and military supremacy over the US.

Kennedy asked Vice President Lyndon Johnson to make recommendations on a scientific endeavour that would prove US world

Figure 5.1: The Changefirst "Wheel": CSF 1 – Shared change purpose

leadership. This led to a series of political decisions that culminated in the successful Apollo programme.

This story demonstrates how a powerful vision – *"put a man on the moon by the end of the decade"* – together with creating real dissatisfaction with the status quo by playing on fears of Soviet dominance were combined to build urgency and momentum for change. This is what we call shared change purpose.

There are three components of a successful shared purpose:

- **Imperative:** people are dissatisfied with their current ways of working and understand the cost if they don't change
- **Vision:** people have a positive and clear picture of the outcomes of the change
- **Solution:** there is a set of milestones to show people how progress will be made

Let's look at these in more detail.

Imperative

Edgar Willie of the Ashridge Research Group investigated 178 organisations from around the world to identify exactly what the triggers for change were. What he found was that:

- 24 per cent of change was instigated as a result of financial loss or drop in profits
- 23 per cent of change was instigated as a result of increased competition or loss of market share
- 23 per cent of change was instigated as a pre-emptive strike by management who foresaw issues arising if they did not change
- 16 per cent of change was instigated as a result of having a new CEO
- 8 per cent of change was instigated as a result of technology
- 6 per cent of change was instigated as a result of recession

With the possible exception of the impact of a new CEO, all the other triggers originate from a realisation that the status quo is no longer good enough. This could be because of unsolved problems or potentially missed opportunities.

If we take it back to the individual for a moment, we know that there is a strong desire to maintain the status quo. In Chapter Two we talked about the power of *"control"* and how it is so important for people to feel a sense of control. The reality is that it is the status quo that gives us that sense of control and comfort. As a result, focusing solely on an attractive vision leaves us unprepared for the inevitable setbacks and barriers we meet during the change process. If a change initiative is to be successful, vision is not enough: you also have to help people see that the status quo is no longer viable for them or their organisation. The desire to not stay where we are can be a more powerful motivator of change than a picture of an attractive future. I remember reading Eric Clapton's autobiography where he talked about his battle to overcome drug and alcohol addiction. He wrote about his vision of being sober, drug free and having a good time with his children. He would paint that picture and, sure enough, he was able to change for a while – but he always relapsed. He didn't begin to really change until he had an *"epiphany"* that he didn't want to be the way he was any more. The status quo was no longer an option. Clapton moved from being temporarily inspired about a future vision to being fully engaged in changing.

A powerful shared change purpose will make people dissatisfied with their current ways of working and allow them to understand the costs associated with not changing. In our experience, it is this imperative that is so frequently missed out of successful change. People are not told why the change is happening. They are not told why it's important for the business and, perhaps most importantly, they are not told why it's important for them individually to get on board. This is at least in part because managers often find the imperative hard to deliver. It feels negative and can create uncertainty, while all of their training tells them to be positive, focus on the vision and appear upbeat. Explaining the imperative for change therefore flies in the face of established management thinking. Yet if people don't know the reasons for change they find it hard to engage, and as soon as inevitable challenges arise in the transition period those affected simply retreat to the way work was done before.

Easy on the imperative!

The crafting of imperatives that work is a potentially difficult task, and you face three potential traps.

The first is that imperative morphs into fear, uncertainty and doubt (FUD) which in turn create immobilisation. You want people to feel that they can't stay where they are. You want them to believe that the current state is an unattractive and untenable place to be, but you don't want to terrify them. You may have experienced a strong sense of wanting to move on in your personal life. Perhaps you have felt like this in a relationship, or even in a house or apartment you were living in. Knowing it's time to make the move is a great first step and a powerful motivator for creating real change. The problem is that when this *"imperative"* turns into fear it creates panic, and panic is unhelpful. Say you decided to move house. Even if you could envision your new place and were really excited about the move, you'd be overwhelmed by the imperative to change if your landlord told you that you had to be out in a week's time as the building was being flattened for development. Your job as a change leader is to move people out of their comfort zone, but not too far. If people become afraid of change and afraid of the status quo, they become immobilised and unable to act. I have seen a number of situations where people in companies feel so threatened both by the change and the imperative to change that they cannot function, and all working time is consumed by informal gatherings at the coffee machine.

Second, you can't turn every change into an *"end of the world"* event; it simply loses the power of the message. I was talking to a mid-level manager one day. He said that the change he was working on at that moment was the fourth time he had been told by senior management that he would be *"outsourced if he didn't pull the change off"*. After the fourth time, this manager neither believed nor cared what senior management said: a clear case of them crying wolf too many times.

Lastly, avoid criticising either the past or any individuals. Doing so will only create resistance. We have probably all seen the *"macho"* manager come in and make pronouncements that he (or she) was going to fix everything that had gone wrong before their arrival. They position themselves as saviours, only to be seen as ungrateful destroyers. I was in an organisation recently where a board level director had come in a few years earlier, told people they had failed and said he was there to fix all their mistakes through his programme of change. Two years later I could still feel the palpable dislike, distrust and anger towards this man. He was a walking, talking resistance creator. The only people who went to his farewell drinks were there to make sure he was really leaving and wasn't coming back!

Vision

Once you have shared the imperative for change, a positive, clear and attractive vision for the future state of the change initiative needs to be put in place. This was well illustrated by the lunar exploration vision that Kennedy painted in 1962. When you listen to his speech there is absolutely no doubt about what would happen if it was successful. The speech was ambitious, unambiguous, concise and clear. More than anything, Kennedy created a picture you could see and imagine. There could never be any debate about when the target was reached; it was self-evident. With the moon landing, people knew that it had been achieved (well, apart from a small minority who thought it was a Hollywood production). Similarly, it acted as a motivator for people, a way they could give meaning to their work. You may have read about the cleaner at NASA who was asked what he did in the organisation and said, *"I am helping to get a man to the moon"*. You want something like this in your change projects. You want people to be motivated and directed by the change vision.

Kennedy's promise to the nation was short and to the point – both enviable qualities. The same applies to any change project: people need to know where you want them to go and why. I remember a client's vision some years ago. It was aimed at a health and safety change initiative in an industry and business that had seen more than its fair share of mortalities. His vision was *"no one killed while I am CEO"*. It was crystal clear and to the point; everyone understood what was required.

For your vision to be seen as strong, your communication to people needs to be clear about the outcomes to be achieved when the change has been delivered, the picture of success when the change has been implemented and how work behaviours will need to be changed.

Kennedy's vision was very compelling and exciting. And wherever you can you should, of course, aim for that. You want people to be excited about your change programme. But that's not always possible. So think of base camp as being *"clarity"*. In fact, it is better for people to be very clear about a change than it is for them to be excited about an unclear, somewhat foggy change definition.

Balancing imperative and vision

We talked about how you need a balance between imperative and vision. Too much imperative, and you cause people to be fearful without them knowing what to do about it. It makes them fall back on old habits rather than embracing the new. Too much vision, and people can become over-optimistic and ignore the true costs of changing, and they seem to be less able to deal with setbacks. Being overly optimistic can be harmful in change situations. Being too optimistic can actually cause you to misjudge what it will take to be successful and can make you less resilient as you try to deal with the inevitable barriers you run into. What seems to work is when you can create a balance between *"this is why we can't stay where we are"* and *"this is where we are heading"*. Somehow managers need to be able to talk about these two thoughts simultaneously. We want people to be realistic about the current state and yet willing to try out new things.

Solution

The shared change purpose should also include the way the change will be achieved. We call this the *"solution"*. People want to know how they are going to get to the vision. Is there a road map which you can give them? If you don't provide this solution you may create more anxiety and concern.

However, there isn't always a solution in this initial stage. Often change becomes necessary without the solution presenting itself so readily. Being open and honest about that in your organisational communication can be beneficial. If you don't know what the solution is, then tell people how the solution will be designed and built. Reassure them that the change process you are using will facilitate the design of the solution. Think carefully how you might want to involve them in doing that. Even if there is no immediate solution to share, people just knowing that there is a process that will give them steps to confidently build the solution is often enough to keep uncertainty and anxiety at bay. Energy and urgency for the change is assisted if people can see the change as possible and understand their role in it.

As part of the solution-building stage remember to pay particular attention to behaviour. Identify what behaviours you need to see more of in the future for the change to be lasting and successful, and which behaviours you need to see less of.

Involve people in creating the solution – when the conversation starts, the change process begins

You have probably noticed an underlying assumption in this book – that the change has been given to you to implement by senior executives. The *"What"* is decided and you now need to implement it. This is because, in our experience, this is what happens in most large organisations and we are trying to provide you with tools and processes to help you with what you need to do. This approach was confirmed by a recent HBR Advisory Council survey in 2010 that showed that 59 per cent of respondents agreed, at least somewhat, with the statement, *"There is an imaginary line in my company's organisation chart. Strategy is created by people above the line, while strategy is executed by people below the line"*. This confirms our perception of what constitutes reality for most people.

The data from the survey then states that the people involved in strategy development are most likely to buy into it, and hence this little diversion I am taking you on. One of the most powerful ways to create commitment to change is by involving people in its creation. This involvement can be done at a local level by techniques such as *"Work-Out"* or *"Appreciative Inquiry"*, or at the organisational level by large-scale organisational planning techniques. We are not particularly concerned with the former at this stage, but let's pause for a moment on the organisational type of interventions.

Additionally, as the title of this section suggests, the moment people hear about a prospective change they start talking, reacting to it and forming views and ideas. There is a huge advantage if you can enlist these people to help you build the solution. You can create some early commitment to the change, rather than resistance.

We have seen large-scale interventions work in changes such as cost cutting, planning mergers and improving organisational performance. They can be very effective where you need people's input and ideas, and where commitment is central to success. They can also create solutions which are easier and better to implement because the people actually doing the jobs have had an input.

Successful large-scale change is often characterised by involving most of the people in the organisation in the process, creating greater speed by having everyone participate at the same time and allowing shared change purpose to develop through the open sharing and synthesising of ideas. Other characteristics include creating a set of solutions with participant ownership and participants seeing their goal as solving real business problems or seizing opportunities.

When done well, all these techniques can create high levels of commitment to change. People always feel more ownership toward things they have helped create. By engaging people right at the start of the process you have the opportunity to create early commitment and reduce potential resistance before it gets started.

But let's get back to shared change purpose.

How to create a shared change purpose

The word *"shared"* is a very important component of this critical success factor. It refers both to the fact that the vision for the future has to be shared with people in the organisation, and also that it is most powerful when created through the sharing of ideas rather than by top-down instructions.

There are two main ways to create a shared change purpose. You can decide on the change purpose yourself and communicate it to others, or you can create the change purpose while working with a wider group of people.

The advantages of *"decide and communicate"* are that it's fast and appears easier, especially if you're already busy with other work. The working assumption is that involvement takes too long, so deciding on the messages and simply announcing those messages can be viewed as the best approach. Problem is, it doesn't work that well unless there is a seriously urgent situation where consultation is impossible. If there was a fire, for example, then you probably wouldn't want to sit around with the fire department deciding what should be done. They'd appreciate a *"decide and communicate"* approach.

For almost everything else, involvement usually delivers a better result. If you create a shared change purpose by getting key people across the organisation together and asking for their input, you will have started the process of achieving buy-in. By involving people in the process you build commitment to the change. People who are consulted often feel more valued and *"heard"* than their colleagues who are simply told.

Which approach you take will depend on the nature of the change and the situation facing the organisation. If you are going into a merger, then it may not be useful or relevant to ask all the employees in the company their opinion. If you are seeking to make changes to business processes then it might make a lot of sense to get people together and involve them.

Here are a few ideas to follow if you want people to have an early buy-in to the change.

Think of using stories rather than bullet points. Bullet points do just that: they shoot communication stone dead. People remember simple stories, and stories have been used for thousands of years to remember and retell events. They are equally as powerful in twenty-first-century organisations as they were in ancient China or Greece. And get people together to create their own stories. We have found that groups of people can be encouraged to describe an organisation's issues and challenges. What is clear from our work is that people value what they create far more highly than what is given to them.

If you can't get people to create their own stories, think about using an elevator speech. This works as a simple, punchy and easy to remember communication of the change. It is a short and focused description of the change told in story format so that it is easy to remember and therefore easy to pass on. Keep it short. A good elevator speech will last less than two minutes, something Mark Twain was obviously familiar with when he wrote, *"Sorry I wrote you a long letter, I didn't have time to write you a short one".*

Start where people are, not where you would like them to be. Danah Zonar, in her book *Re-wiring the Corporate Brain: Using the New Science to Rethink How We Structure and Lead Organizations*, found that different people are motivated by different issues. These motivations are fairly evenly split between impacts on society, customers, the organisation, working teams and themselves. If you are motivated by the impact on your customers, then the story or elevator speech that is going to motivate you to get on board is the version that puts the change in that context. If you are more focused on working teams, then the elevator speech would include how they would be affected by the change. Use this information to shape your messages by finding out what people's *"hot buttons"* are. This means you need to vary the elevator speech depending on who you are speaking to and on their area of motivation. Tap into their interests, not yours.

Structure messages and conversations in different ways to suit individuals and groups. Paul Mok, in his work on communication styles, identified four communication preferences: Sensors (people who like short, action-oriented communications); Feelers (people who prefer to hear about people and the affects of change on people); Thinkers (people who like steps and processes) and Intuitors (those who like to see the big picture).

Use symbols to communicate that change is happening and forget the slides. I came across the regional head of a computer company some years ago who told me how he had driven a change to make the organisation less bureaucratic and rule-bound – so he organised a *"funeral"* with a proper wake. People came and burned the old rule books and policy manuals. They then told stories about the people who had worked there, told jokes about how rules had been bent and generally drank too much wine. The next morning he told them that this was history and they all – including him – needed to move on. It all sounds very rather *"soft"* but it worked. The sheer symbolism gripped people in a way that forty slides never would.

Key actions for creating shared change purpose

You will need to make some decisions around involvement and approval. The questions you need to answer in this early process are these:

1. Who will be involved in building the shared change purpose? As we have already discussed, people tend to buy into changes that they have had a part in creating. Is this an early opportunity – even if the change has been decided on – to engage people in the change?

2. Can you road-test the shared change purpose? Be careful to pilot messages and approaches. What can sound great in the project planning office can sound insensitive and irrelevant when you deliver it at a manufacturing site or in a call centre.

3. Who needs to approve it? Always, always make sure the steering team or executive group are committed to what you are going to say or do. My advice would be to use the 80 per cent accurate/100 per cent committed rule. It's much better for the executives to have a message that they are committed to and willing to communicate, than it is to try and force them to use a *"technically more accurate"* message that they are not committed to because it's not *"theirs"*.

4. How will you roll it out? The great temptation, particularly in large organisations, is to tell people. We have seen this done by email, slides and even by text messaging. We will talk about this later, but do try and use face-to-face communication. If you are in a large organisation then this has to be done by cascading the messages. In smaller organisations you might be able to speak to everyone personally.

At this point in the change cycle, think of yourself as a salesperson. You are trying to sell the idea to others. Successful salespeople rarely tell their customers what to do. They involve them, seek out their perspectives, use multiple communication channels and often get the customer to help them build the solution. They know that *"pull"* works far better than "*push*".

A well-crafted shared change purpose helps people to stay motivated through the transition period because it develops urgency, energy and clarity – all of which create momentum for change. If genuinely shared, it can pull people forward and helps them resist the temptation of slipping back into comfortable old habits. Shared change purpose acts as a way of galvanising the change, is often the first demonstration of cooperation and a demonstration of the level of shared agreement necessary to pull it off. And finally, a compelling and powerful shared change purpose guides behaviour and actions at both an organisational and local level to achieve successful change implementation.

Now it's time to build effective change leadership.

6

Building effective change leadership – enrolling key leaders

At Changefirst we train hundreds of change agents every year and there is one consistent comment that is made at every workshop: *"I thought I would spend a lot of time with front-line workers helping them to adopt the change. But I actually spend the majority of my time coordinating managers and executives to visibly support the change."* Or, sometimes, *"What tips do you have for getting management attention to the change they asked me to deliver?"*

What these fraught individuals are almost always wrestling with is how to be strong change leaders in the face of resistance or opposition, especially when that resistance or opposition comes from those more senior than they are. The assumption they often mistakenly arrive at is that they must be poor change leaders – otherwise they would successfully get the management's attention.

Is it that strong change leaders are a rare and elusive breed? Is it that successful change is just so difficult that few reach the required benchmark? Is it that strong change leadership is an innate quality that you either have or don't have? Or is it just down to a lack of skill?

One of the ongoing highlights of my career is that I have had the privilege of working with some great change leaders. They have cropped up everywhere – executives, project leaders, middle managers and

Figure 6.1: The Changefirst "Wheel": CSF 2 – Effective change leadership

front-line managers. And I've learned a lot from watching them over the years. But the biggest lesson I've learned is that strong change leadership is not rare, it's not an innate gift that only a few possess and it's not an impossible challenge. It all comes down to skill. And that skill can be learned.

Concerns about how to secure effective change leadership are echoed by most of the research over the last thirty years, and it is often cited as the number one risk factor in major change. In 2009 we commissioned *Change in a Downturn* – a survey which was sent to 2000 participants across 26 countries. The results indicated that effective change leadership is very often seen as the root problem of unsuccessful change. In many respects this is another really obvious aspect of successful change; after all, well-led change will almost always be better than poorly led change. Sadly, as results will attest, the obvious doesn't necessarily translate into constructive solutions and action. This paradox is one of the great corporate mysteries: why is it that leaders who initiate change then go on to ignore it? They certainly don't do everything they can to make sure it is implemented.

Effective change leadership happens when the leaders of change provide direction, guidance and support to the people who are implementing change, as well as those affected by and working with the change on a daily basis.

The three main change leadership roles

In most change projects there are three main change leadership roles that are necessary: sponsors, influencers and change agents. Without clarity about who is doing what and who is responsible for what, nothing will ever get done. This is as true for change management as is for any other business process. Let's look at the three roles, briefly at first and then in more detail.

Sponsors are accountable for the successful implementation of the change in their area of responsibility. It is up to these people to ensure that the benefits of change are fully realised. Don't confuse this role with titles like *"Project Champion"* or *"Executive Sponsor"*. We use the term to mean all the people who have accountability for making a change happen. In successful major change there are usually multiple sponsors who are networking the change and cascading it down through the organisation.

Influencers wield significant informal power. One definition of influence is, *"the power to affect, control or manipulate something or someone; the ability to change the development of fluctuating things such as conduct, thoughts or decisions; an action exerted by a person or thing with such power on another to cause change; a person or thing exerting such power or action"*. The key point in all of these is informal power. In other words, influencers can't direct people to do something – but they exert a different type of power which is equally, if not more, important.

Change agents work with sponsors to plan and execute the tasks or activities that enable people to adapt to the change and ensure that it is fully implemented, as opposed to installed and forgotten. They rarely have sufficient formal power and are therefore reliant on persuading and working with others to make change happen.

To build further clarification of the different roles let's apply them to a change project. Say, for example, that a large distribution company recognised the need for major change to its network. Complaints were on the rise, competition was tightening and customers were becoming increasingly discerning about what they wanted as part of regular service. It was clear that nothing short of a total overhaul of the supply chain would do. Greater integration between the 30 distribution centres and a better tracking system to manage the flow of goods through to the customer needed to be implemented.

Who are the sponsors here? The sponsors for this change would include the Vice President (VP) of Logistics, as she has to drive the changes that would impact her distribution network. The VP's actions are further strengthened by another layer of sponsors, who are the General Managers of each of the regions. They need to make sure the Distribution Centre Managers are on board, committed and able to lead the change effectively. Then each of these centre managers needs to be a sponsor. In truth, every manager who has to ensure the change happens is a sponsor.

And who are the agents? The agent will probably be a Project or Line Manager who is assigned to the project. He will be told to *"lead"* it, but in reality will build the plan, coordinate roll-out activities, deal with problems and keep track. This Project or Line Manager will work alongside the Logistics VP and she will ensure he gets the support he needs to be successful. There will be another layer of agents who have been selected in each region or distribution centre. These agents would be working with their individual General Managers to build local plans and execute tasks that will impact their colleagues on the floor.

Who are the influencers? As soon as it became obvious that change was going to be necessary to improve distribution performance, the VP of Logistics knew that she needed to involve Bob Scott, the well-respected Distribution Manager for the largest centre, who had been with the company for 15 years. Half a dozen other influencers were identified and brought into the core team.

And, of course, change leaders can play multiple roles at any one time. For example, a Chief Information Officer (CIO) can be a sponsor for change in his or her team, but when it comes to implementing major IT change across the organisation the CIO is a change agent. This is important because it determines how people need to behave in different roles. In the agent role the CIO would probably need to spend far more time persuading, facilitating and consulting than in the sponsor role.

If you want to be effective you need to ensure that everyone understands the different roles they need to play and how you can help them be effective in those roles. You should try and achieve this very early in the change process. A Changefirst technique known as *"Change Network Mapping"* can help you identify these roles and who the key players are. In addition it will help you understand the communications, relationships and power dynamics between them all.

Now let's look at the three roles in more depth.

What makes an effective sponsor

Sometimes ideas and directives are handed down from executives like proverbial hot potatoes. As soon as the hot potato is offloaded the sponsor will disappear and can be hard to pin down. However, effective change is only possible when the sponsors of the change are actively involved in the change and their commitment is clear to others.

It's an important part of your job to help sponsors be as successful as possible. Even sponsors with the best of intentions can be ineffective. If they are unclear about their role during implementation they may not be able to provide the support that people need. For the last 15 years we have been collecting data and information on what makes sponsors successful, and the result is a tool that tracks 12 dimensions of effective sponsorship. I want to highlight three of the dimensions that we think are particularly important for sponsors.

Firstly, great sponsors lead by *"doing"*. During change, people seem to notice almost every gap between what sponsors say and what they do. I remember, some ten years ago, trying to coach an executive team when they were trying to cut costs and increase operating efficiencies. This project was going to take about two years to complete. They were working with a major consulting firm on the process redesign parts of the project, and actually it was going well. However, I had already had some conversations about their habit of flying first class and how this had been commented on by groups of middle managers in focus groups we had held. The executive team members told me that *"these people"* didn't understand how much they all travelled and how tiring it was. About a third of the way into the project they decided that the senior managers' car policy (including their own) was uncompetitive and was stopping them hiring the *"right"* people. I couldn't understand why you would want people in your organisation who would be put off joining you because of the type of car they would get – but much, much more importantly I highlighted the symbolism of this at a time of huge cost constraint. The CEO told me that he was *"running a business not a theatre"*. He didn't need to justify his decisions nor did he need to use *"pointless symbols"* to make his point. Suffice to say that the cost cutting didn't achieve its goals and that the CEO was removed soon afterwards. The people in the organisation just didn't believe that management were serious about cost reduction and resented the inequalities they observed. As one middle manager said to me: *"So they cancelled the free coffee to pay for a better Lexus!"*

Contrast this with an example I was given by a participant in a workshop. I asked the group for positive examples of active leadership. One of the participants said this: *"We have a project that is experiencing some difficulties and we had to work over the weekend because of errors and mistakes the system made. On the Saturday the senior executive responsible for the project joined us at eight in the morning, sat down, picked up a pile of error reports and worked through the pile until five in the afternoon. He acted as if he was just one of the project team. He then got us all together on Monday to help build a more solid plan for dealing with the problems. The key point was that my project team was just so motivated by this simple action. He was there helping us, not on his BlackBerry demanding project updates."*

Secondly, strong sponsors communicate consistently and congruently about the change. This covers a number of aspects. They communicate consistently when they are in public and they are just as passionate and resolute in private. They track milestones and progress. They are open to feedback from anyone involved in the change. In fact, they relish it. A great example of this is a change leader I'll call Linda. Linda was absolutely consistent in what she said to you about the change, regardless of whether you were on your own or in a group. She was also very open to feedback; she seemed to thrive on it. Every time I saw her in action I was reminded of the old cliché that *"change is a contact sport"*. She seemed to love debating with people about the change, and saw every exchange as a chance to sell the change. Like a talented salesperson, she saw objections as an opportunity to resell her message. Now, this didn't convert everyone into an evangelist for the change – but in political terms it consolidated the base, converted a few non-believers and the opposition saw that she was passionate about the change. They were dealing with a resolute person. Not everyone can be like Linda, but change leaders can be helped to be consistent, to be disciplined and not to back-track without realising it.

Lastly, successful sponsors build a strong network of other sponsors. We have already talked about the importance of building a strong sponsor network. You need to find ways to share information effectively, cascade communication through the organisation, and exert power and influence to ensure the change can be fully implemented across the board.

This aspect of a sponsor's role has become increasingly important as the nature and structure of business operations has changed. Organisations have changed in some ways since the 1980s. In particular, we now see more organisations using a matrix framework as opposed to the more traditional hierarchies. There are often more interim employees and sometimes the differences between consultants, contractors and full-time employees become blurred. Organisations are sometimes rebuilt around process. Regional organisations sometimes disappear to be replaced by global business units. Techniques such as lean manufacturing have already delayered many manufacturing organisations. This global restructuring, downsizing, re-engineering, etc, has led to speculation that hierarchies are dead and formal organisation power is no longer what it was. When you orchestrate major change be very careful of this assumption. There is always a lot of talk about something called *"bottom-up change"*. I have never seen it, unless you mean some of the solution-building techniques we discussed earlier. Ignore formal organisation power at your peril. Harold Leavitt, in his book *Top Down*, suggests that not much has really changed in large organisations. He argues that basically the average organisation is as hierarchical as ever and that, contrary to predictions, virtual working has not fundamentally changed the way we work. If Leavitt is right – and I think he is – you should take traditional power and politics very seriously when you plan major change. Traditional hierarchies may still be in place, but demanding change from the top-down doesn't work. Bottom-up change is largely a myth, so finding a balance is essential. Most change agents report that in the majority of cases cascading change from the top to the bottom of the organisation is still the most effective way to deploy change. Not enough on its own but, nevertheless, critical.

We worked with a major multinational IT organisation, for example, that began implementing new selling processes and technology across its Europe, Middle East and Africa region (EMEA). While the change was initiated in the US head office, and was actively being managed out of the EMEA centre, the decentralised culture of this business meant that each of the EMEA countries operated as independent fiefdoms. This meant that in reality the regional and country heads could – formally or informally – veto a demand for change as long as they continued to meet financial targets.

As a consequence there wasn't a sufficiently strong sponsor network. For this change to be successful the regional and country managers needed to be enrolled, the influence of major sales managers and personnel had to be used to build champions for the change and critical change communications had to be delivered by the local business head.

To ensure this happened, the main change agent built a process that went country by country to build support for the change. A series of workshops were held that enabled each country's management team to buy into the change and then to plan a specific implementation in their own particular country. This led to very high ownership of both the change and the method of implementation. The agent was smart enough to understand that all sponsors needed to be committed and that, because of the organisational culture, only an engaging process would work.

How to build a strong sponsor network
You have a limited number of tools at your disposal to help you build the network.

Involvement is the first. The best way to engage sponsors is by involving them. This is what the change agent did in the case study above. You can involve managers in the design of how the change will unfold in their area and how it will be implemented. You should be thoughtful about who you involve in the early stages of the change. If an area is going to be heavily affected, then bring a sponsor from that area into the project or steering team. If sponsors feel part of the decision-making processes their commitment to the change will quickly grow. You should always endeavour to use involvement first.

Persuasion is the next tool to use. If involvement does not work or just isn't possible, the next method is to try and convince the sponsor of the benefits of the change. We have seen this work many times in practice. A change agent we trained set up a whole series of one-on-one meetings between the initiating sponsor (in this case the CEO) and key sponsors further down the organisation. These meetings allowed the most powerful person in the organisation – the CEO – to put the case to unconvinced leaders. This approach allowed him to successfully win over the others so they could move the change forward to implementation.

Next come rewards. If participation and persuasion don't work, the next possible option is using rewards. These rewards can be generally targeted at a group through, for example, the resetting of key performance targets. We have also seen the successful use of smaller, less formal rewards to get the point across. Freud told us that people are motivated towards pleasure and away from pain, so bringing in incentives for correct behaviour can help facilitate a more rapid assimilation of the new behaviour.

Finally, there's Isolation. If all else fails then it may be necessary to work around those sponsors who are working against the change. This may mean reassigning the particular sponsor to another position, removing responsibilities and authority for the business outcomes affected by the change or even, in extreme cases, dismissal. If you don't have the power to do this you might find ways to work around people or to move them out of the process. I once disinvited a couple of managers from a weekly project planning meeting – frankly, I was bored with dealing with them and their continual slowing down of the change process. When they asked me why they were not included, I told them that they were clearly opposed to the change and it seemed a waste of everyone's time, including their own, for them to attend. This had a strange cathartic effect which I hadn't expected. For them, it was a turning point, and they came back some weeks later much more supportive of the change.

This is probably one of the biggest issues we face. A change agent we trained in our change process faced this situation when trying to implement a really significant change across her organisation. She had built a reasonable network of support among sponsors. However, a senior manager in a key part of the organisation kept saying that he supported the change but then did nothing to implement it. Despite spending time with the manager and then finally going to his boss, nothing happened. The boss, when finally confronted with the issue, pointed out that the manager was great at his day job and said that he wasn't prepared to lose him over his resistance to the change. This forced the change agent to retreat and try to find a way to work around that part of the organisation; ultimately, however, the change was less successful than it might have been. In hindsight she had missed a vital signal from the boss – as far as he was concerned this change was not as important as the performance of the manager in his day job. What this case highlights is how hard it is when credible and talented managers block your change efforts. If the initiating sponsor is not prepared to take action then you have to try and isolate the person concerned. They may eventually come on board because a critical mass forms among their peers but, in our experience, this is not always the case. This can force sponsors into tough choices about how important the change is versus keeping key individuals.

What makes an effective influencer

Change is much more likely to succeed when it is backed by clear, active support from other influential people in the organisation. The role of influential people has always been important in change but it has grown exponentially so with the advancement of communication technology. Communication changes like email, intranet sites and social networking have made it far easier to network with others right across the globe. As such, these individuals are wielding even more sway as their influence can be disseminated across an organisation through a variety of new technological means. The role influencers play in making change happen was the subject of Malcolm Gladwell's bestselling book *The Tipping Point: How Little Things Can Make a Big Difference*. This book basically summarised, in a very readable way, much of the supporting evidence on the role that influencers play.

It was renowned sociologist Stanley Milgram who helped us understand this dynamic a little more. In one set of experiments Milgram demonstrated what later became known as the *"small world phenomenon"*. He wanted to know how connected we all are. He devised an experiment in which he gave a letter to someone in Nebraska. That person was told that the letter had to reach a particular person in Massachusetts whom they did not know. The first sender was given only basic facts about the end target, such as occupation, and from that information they had to send the letter on to someone they knew on a first-name basis who had to do the same thing in order for the letter to reach its final destination. On average, Milgram found that the letter was sent six times before it reached its destination. This is the basis of the well-known idea of six degrees of separation. This means that whoever you are and wherever you are, you and I are separated by only six people or degrees of separation. That's not that many, and illustrates just how connected we all are.

Later work has built on this and shows that not only are we more connected than we might imagine, but that our levels of trust are affected by these degrees of separation. Not only do we trust people who are directly connected to us, but we also trust people who are maybe two or even three separations away. In her book *Web 2.0: A Strategy Guide*, Amy Shuen suggests that the explosion of social networking and user-participation technology means that we are relying on these connections far more than on traditional authority figures or even advertising to make our decisions. Although she points out that trust in the connection drops with each degree, the scope of contacts makes up for it. So, for example, if you recommended your friend Susan for a job I'd trust your judgement and interview Susan; if you said that Susan knew someone else who would be great for the job my trust levels would start to fall. I don't know Susan and although I can make a judgement about her based on my experience of you (birds of a feather flock together), I can't necessarily make that judgement about someone who is two steps removed. Technology, however, allows us to connect to far more people than before and use that technology to build those trust levels beyond the usual two or three degrees of separation in the offline world. For example, the business networking website LinkedIn allows contacts to add endorsements and testimonials. This is proving to build trust further than the offline norm of two to three degrees of separation. In fact, of the 25,000 requests for introduction in mid-2005, 87 per cent were accepted. These types of connections are getting things done.

In our work inside organisations, we have identified four types of influencers:

- **Advocates:** these are people who can potentially persuade others about the benefits of the change. It's very important to work with them early in the process. You need to plant ideas with them and turn them into early adopters

- **Connectors:** they help you reach others in the network that you might want to influence. They help you find allies and enlist support. They can also help you develop a critical mass of key people in favour of the change

- **Controllers:** they control access to people and information. They may not be very senior; in fact, many of them may be in mid-level staff roles. But they need cultivating and they need to understand how they can help you

- **Experts:** they are recognised as being technically credible by others in the organisation. Remember they may not actually be technical experts; it's just that others regard them as so

You need to identify and understand the role that each of these influencers plays. They all have influence but you will need their assistance at different times in the change process. The more you understand your organisation and the people in it, the easier this becomes. In one of our client organisations, the CEO and a factory manager located in China had both started work for the company as trainees 25 years earlier. Before the CEO began his rapid climb up the organisation they shared many experiences, both good and bad, that bonded them. Unless you knew the organisation really well you wouldn't know about this relationship. Every time the CEO wanted to take the company pulse about a change he would call the factory manager and ask him what he thought. Wise change agents would treat the manager as a potential advocate and get to him first. So if you don't know about the history and politics of the organisation, then either find out or bring someone onto your team who does.

Put bluntly, you have to pay more attention to some people in the change process than others. When you stop and think about it, you already know that some people in the organisation have more influence than others. You know this instinctively and need to bring that knowledge into the change process to initiate effective change leadership.

What makes an effective change agent

It was 1989 and I was driving up Route 101 in Northern California. It was 7 am in the morning. I hadn't slept well that night. Some months before I had been transferred from our UK offices to a US subsidiary. It was an insurance company based in California that had been in decline for some time and needed transforming into something more relevant, profitable and vibrant. It had all started so well. My executive colleagues had been very welcoming, there was a huge imperative for change and my family had settled into what was hardly a hardship posting. It was my first big change agent role, and what I lacked in skills and experience I made up for in energy and willingness to make a difference. But I had woken up this particular morning at about 2 am, full of anxiety and concern. My boss was supportive but thought I could achieve more through my personal interventions than working through my colleagues. My colleagues had started to resist the change as they realised what it meant to them personally. Co-workers mistook my support for my boss in public with a lack of challenge to her in private, and so thought I was simply her cipher. The project was slowing as middle managers also began to resist, and an alliance of these managers and some long-service executives threatened to derail the effort entirely. On top of that, some of the early IT changes were malfunctioning and proving tougher to implement than we had first thought. This had a snowball effect, as it meant we couldn't make some of the other changes we wanted to implement. Then I realised what had happened: I was living through what people had predicted would happen to me. I had become a change agent. It is a role I have lived with in various guises since that time. I realised that my job was to plan and help execute change. I couldn't do it for other people. I didn't have much formal authority and I had to facilitate change rather than order it up. I had to pull (rather than push) people through change wherever possible. And, if that wasn't possible, I needed a plan B (which might be hard to identify).

In the same way that we've developed a sponsor assessment tool, we have also developed an assessment that allows organisations to identify and develop change agents. Of the various dimensions identified, three are absolutely critical for success. Firstly, if you want to be a change agent you have to have a basic level of credibility and trust within the organisation. Some years ago we were asked to visit an organisation that had launched a £10 million IT change. The change had ground the organisation to an absolute halt. They were losing customers and key staff on an hourly basis. I met the main change agent briefly. He was a pleasant person with good intentions but lacked many of the skills that change agents need. He wasn't a good facilitator, he couldn't influence people, he selected poor support staff but, more than anything, he also lacked credibility in key parts of the organisation. The critical sales organisation didn't see him as someone who could help them change their organisation, and the net result was that they resisted almost anything he proposed. The change couldn't recover until he was gone. He was replaced with a manager from the sales team whom the whole organisation respected and trusted. It was one of the most critical factors in re-energising the change.

Secondly, change agents need to be able to challenge up, across and down the organisation. What will often happen in major change projects is that people are so busy and working so hard that they stop listening and observing what is really happening. This means that some of the decisions they make are based on false premises or inaccurate information. The person who can counter this is the change agent. The ability to confront people without alienating them is a very difficult skill to master. In my experience you need to have close personal relationships with senior sponsors to achieve this. They need to value feedback from you. They may not like hearing negative feedback, but they may listen if they respect you and if you have shown that you can be trusted. If this is the first time working with a sponsor, start with technical and more general change issues. Keep your challenges small. Let trust build up. What you will find is that over time you can escalate the feedback as trust develops. Once this trust is built up, you should be able to talk about your role as a change agent and the impact the sponsor team is having on change performance. Once that has created a relationship, you can begin to help the sponsor with their own performance. Remember the old feedback rule: if you have to tell someone one bad thing, then give them three good things to counter the negative. This system is far from perfect, but it can help take the sting out of the feedback and allow the individual to rectify the issue without feeling incompetent.

Some executives, however, refuse to listen to any negative feedback. They can find it threatening and may even see it as *"insubordination"*. In my experience you can do little about these people and you should either try and work around them or prepare for the project to sub-optimise. In other words, if you can, run for the hills!

Thirdly, learn some influencing skills. I know selling feels an inappropriate word for some of you. But that's part of your job. One of the biggest mistakes I see change agents making is to perceive their role as a technical one: *"My job is to make sure there is a plan and track it. I can't influence people. And anyway that's not my job."* Your potential success is based on your ability to work with the channels of power and influence that affect the project. If you need a primer for this, one of the best pieces I have ever read on this subject is a Harvard Business Review article called *"Breakthrough Bargaining"* by Kolb and Williams. It talks about the strategies you can deploy when people hold unequal power. Every change agent I have ever recommended this article to has found it useful in some way. Kolb and Williams talk about ways to coax people to participate, how to shape the way decisions are made and how to make it feel safe for people to participate in your project.

Key actions for building effective change leadership

The questions you need to answer to build effective change leadership are these:

1. Have you identified the leaders who will be able to help you make the project a success? Early on in the project you could be assigned certain people or told certain individuals will be crucial. Listen to all of the opinions and then make your own decisions about who you need to enrol into the change.

2. Have you built early support for what will have to be done if this project is to be successful? It's usually far more effective if you engage with key leaders – they could be sponsors, influencers or other agents – early in the change process. Engage with them before they build a strong view about the change.

3. Do key leaders have the skills and desire to be successful and to support you? If not, then you need to try and fix it. In my experience leaders are often unwilling to admit to a lack of skill, and yet it is this lack of skill that then manifests itself as a low desire to change. So start with some subtle skill building so that key leaders are reassured that they have the skills necessary for change. That way they are much more likely to get behind both you and the change.

4. Have you prepared yourself to lead this change? Change is full of uncertainty, ambiguity and can take a toll on you even if you are prepared. Think about how you could enhance your own skills, mindset and resilience before you start. Most importantly, take some time for yourself. You need to have some time to reflect and recharge your batteries.

Effective change leadership is the first real-world step towards change after the shared change purpose has been decided upon. People are much more likely to support a change initiative when they see the people leading the change *"walking the talk"*. In fact, I'd go so far as to say that unless the change leadership is exhibiting the behaviours they seek from others than the change will never reach its business case potential. This hands-on demonstration of the change helps people overcome the inevitable difficulties that come with adjusting to change: the often-unconscious thought processes say, *"Well, if X or Y can do it, so can I"*. Once you have strong change leadership for the initiative, you can begin the process of rolling out powerful engagement processes.

7

Powerful engagement processes – engaging the organisation

A fairly standard definition of engagement is, *"an employee's involvement with, commitment to, and satisfaction with work"*. Studies have connected high levels of employee engagement to better organisational performance. For example, UK researcher Nancy Lockwood found that employees with the highest level of commitment performed 20 per cent better than their colleagues, and were 87 per cent less likely to leave their organisation.

In change implementation, engagement processes are designed to foster commitment, encourage new behaviours and teach new skills. We have rarely seen commitment built without engaging people in some way or other. The exceptions are where the organisation has an extraordinarily strong imperative. This is usually seen at either end of its lifecycle – in other words, at start-up or when the operation is going out of business unless rapid radical action is taken. When we developed the PCI methodology we could have put this critical success factor right at the centre, instead of organisation and local, because it influences the other five success factors so heavily. Powerful engagement processes are central to successful change.

The four components of a powerful engagement process are:

- Involvement
- Learning
- Rewards
- Communication

Involvement

In 1975 a famous study led by Ellen Langer demonstrated the importance of self-selected involvement. Researchers sold $1 lottery tickets to a selection of participants. In one group the tickets were handed to the participants randomly while people in the other group were allowed to choose their own. A few days later Langer returned to the subjects and asked to buy back the tickets. The ticket holders who had been given a random ticket were willing to sell their ticket, on average, for $2. Those who had chosen their own ticket, on the other hand, wanted on average $9 for their $1 ticket. Langer attributed this to an illusion of control caused by *"an expectancy of a personal success probability inappropriately higher than the objective probability would warrant"*.

We could draw two conclusions from this study. Firstly, people value what they get to choose more highly than something given to them without their input by a ratio of about 4 to 1. Secondly, illusion or not, control matters and involvement can be a very powerful way to give people that sense of control. And this is what involvement creates in change: ownership and control.

As well as helping people to maintain a sense of control, involvement is important for successful change because you can create buy-in to the change. People are far more likely to adopt a process that they have had a part in designing. Years ago we used to do more consulting than we do now. One of the services we used to offer was a *"change repair shop"*. Basically organisations would come to us if their change was not working and ask for assistance to get it back on track again. We would always ask

Figure 7.1: The Changefirst "Wheel": CSF 3 – Powerful engagement
processes

the client if they had consulted with the people affected by the change to
see what difficulties they were having and why those people thought the
change wasn't working. Almost without exception the answer was *"no"*.
Invariably the client was unwilling to go back and take this crucial next
step, so we would do it for them. We would go straight to the people most
affected by the change and ask them, in small groups, what difficulties
they were having and why they thought the change wasn't working. They
would almost always be able to tell us very clearly what was wrong with
the change and – more importantly – how it could be fixed. In about
three-quarters of the cases all we had to do was build an implementation
process around their views. So we have had warehouse staff designing
their own implementation programme, sales people designing a CRM
roll out, cross-functional teams re-designing business processes and
executives analysing what went wrong. That's what involvement is all
about. It's about engaging people to own and accelerate the change.
Plus, this has the positive knock-on effect of making employees feel more
valued and engaged with the organisation.

And incidentally that's why we moved out of the consultancy space. These organisations and the people in them already knew what needed to change; we didn't need to ride in on a white charger and save the day. Sure, we could have taken the credit and the cash and left in a blaze of glory, but the true credit belonged with the people in the business. They knew the solutions before we even arrived; it was just that no one had asked them. Why employ consultants to tell you what your people already know? What organisations really need is to develop change capability so they can structure a proven system around any change and achieve success. And that's exactly what PCI does.

As well as improving buy-in you can actually improve the quality of the change. Two heads (or more) are almost always better than one. Trying to implement a change on your own by telling people doesn't account for other perspectives that could be really crucial in the success of the change. Assuming you know all the answers is rarely useful in creating lasting change or creating a lasting business.

The assumption is that involvement takes forever, but involvement can actually be quicker than telling people – although it took me a long time to realise this. My epiphany arrived one sunny afternoon in San Diego. I was on the harbour with my old company. We were to spend the afternoon racing the America's Cup yachts ourselves; half of the crew of each yacht was replaced by company employees. I was given the job of *"strategist"*. As the strategist I wasn't to worry about how the boat was going or how fast it was travelling, but had to work out our general racing strategy and plan the turns. On the first race we were ahead and we were coming toward the harbour wall. So I signalled to turn – *"30-20-10-turn!"* – but, out of nowhere, the other boat which had been behind us suddenly landed up in front of us coming back. The afternoon was the best of three races, so after the first one the captain called everyone together to regroup and analyse what had gone wrong. A key factor in this sport is that you only have about thirty seconds to make a decision to turn. As the post-mortem began the captain asked me, *"What went wrong?"* I said, *"I don't know; we just seemed really slow to turn."*

Then the captain went around everyone else in the team and asked them the same question. The answer, to a person, was *"David didn't consult with us"*. The captain then asked, *"So what are the implications of that?"* Everyone agreed that it meant they'd not been ready. I was obviously on the back foot a little so I asked, *"But how can I consult with you in thirty seconds?"* The suggestion was made that I simply went round the boat and asked everyone if they were ready and whether the time was right. I agreed to try it.

We set off for race two and as we were approaching the harbour wall, about sixty seconds out, I went round all sixteen crew members and asked if they were ready. Then *"30-20-10-turn!"* – and we won the race, and we won the next race as well. It was a good lesson for me about engaging people. It wasn't about lack of time or ease, it was all about my mindset and willingness to listen. In truth, I didn't consult with them, I didn't engage in a long debate about what needed to be done – I just involved them and made them feel part of the process. And that's the same in business. Often change agents shy away from consultation because it sounds too much like hard work. But, as my experience on the yacht showed me, it doesn't have to be that way.

Time and again we have seen change accelerate through involvement, rather than slow down. Involvement creates momentum that in turn keeps the change moving forward. This is supported by some Ernst and Young research into process re-engineering from the late 1990s. It showed that when involvement was high at the design and implementation stages of the change then change implementation was faster.

Involving people creates higher overall levels of employee engagement and probably adds to people's sum total of feeling engaged with the organisation. In other words, their loyalty and *"stickiness"* to the company is developed, their sense of belonging is assisted and they feel valued. This can be particularly important during change when feelings of uncertainty are high. If people feel a degree of loyalty to the organisation and feel valued and appreciated through the design process, they are far more likely to accommodate the changes and help others to do the same. They get on your side.

How to involve people successfully

There are some critical factors or principles to think about. Let's run through them.

Are your sponsors willing to involve others? For involvement to be successful, leaders have to enter into involvement strategies willingly. In the worst case you have to accept that some people will never get it; they will always consider involvement to be a complete waste of time. They believe that people will tell them what they want to hear, that it will take too long, that people won't have the skills or that involvement will just be too difficult. These are attitudes that might be hard to shift. If you expect the process to be a waste of time, then the chances are it will be. It was sociologist Robert Merton who coined the term *"self-fulfilling prophecy"*. In his book *Social Theory and Social Structure* he states, *"The self-fulfilling prophecy is, in the beginning, a false definition of the situation evoking a new behaviour which makes the original false conception come true. This specious validity of the self-fulfilling prophecy perpetuates a reign of error. For the prophet will cite the actual course of events as proof that he was right from the very beginning."* In other words, if you make up your mind that involvement and consultation is a waste of time you will inadvertently alter your behaviour and actions. You'll engage in it half-heartedly or loaded with cynicism, which will ensure that it's a waste of time. Then you will happily preach to anyone who will listen just how *"right"* you were all along.

Is the timing right and is this an issue that people can help with? If you are going to make an acquisition then you probably don't want to go and ask all the employees in the company their opinion: *"Should we make this acquisition? What do you think about our growth strategy?"* But, time and again, post-merger joint teams from both organisations coming together on specific issues have proved to be highly effective.

Do you have a business issue or problem that needs resolving? In the course of my work I attend quite a few company conferences. There's always that horrible moment when a facilitator says, *"Right, we assigned each table a flipchart and we want you to write down all your ideas for X, Y or Z and we will feed these into the organisational planning process."* Everybody in that room over 30 years of age knows they are about to waste an hour of their life. They will never see or hear about that list again. What's worse is that they could be asked the same question next year. This is typical of where involvement can go wrong. It needs to be focused on a real business issue. People should be asked to produce something that will solve that issue, and they should be told what happened to their work if it's not immediately obvious. Trying to involve people in generic *"room for improvement"* discussions is a waste of time. Only involve people when it's meaningful and something concrete is going to come out of the discussions. Research at the end of the 1990s by the UK's Business Intelligence organisation showed that about 90 per cent of Total Quality Management (TQM) initiatives failed to deliver benefit to the organisations concerned. The main reason was too many projects, too many ideas and too few of these ideas implemented by the organisation, leading to employee cynicism and management resistance.

In his 1990 book *"Hocus Pocus"*, Kurt Vonnegut wrote, *"People are never stronger than when they have thought up their own arguments for believing what they believe. They stand on their own two feet that way."* Somehow there is a simple human truth that people want and like to be involved in issues that affect them. Successful involvement increases ownership and the perception of control, and builds real commitment. Our challenge is to find ways to achieve this in major change.

Learning

I recently went to visit a company which was going through a substantial technology-led change. When walking around with my host we came across a fairly typical classroom with participants sitting at tables in a U-shape facing the instructor at the front of the class. He was doing his best with over 200 slides.

You probably know the presentation well: loads of bullet points and complex diagrams crammed in as if leaving any part of the slide empty was some kind of sin. The participants were learning about *"the system"*. When I asked to see the agenda it became pretty clear that they were going through two days of heavy technical training with little focus on the behaviours they would need to be successful, no attempts to build their commitment to the change and a massive assumption that the participants would be able to start performing the following week when the system was installed. Nobody, least of all the instructor, looked very confident that it was going to happen with any degree of success.

Most changes require new skills and attitudes that people need to learn. However, learning can be a barrier to change as well. Ed Schein, one of the great contributors to organisational psychology, refers to this as learning anxiety and survival anxiety. Learning anxiety comes from being afraid to try something new for fear that it will be too difficult, that we will look foolish in front of our peers or that we will have to part with old ways of working that have served us well. Learning anxiety can therefore threaten our self-esteem.

By giving people enough time to learn you reduce learning anxieties and allow individuals time to adjust and improve to a point when they no longer feel so threatened. Expecting people to learn new skills almost overnight and become proficient in those skills within a week or two is unreasonable. You have to give people the room to adapt, experiment and improve without the pressure of assessment.

How to make learning work for you

Try and make sure that the imperative to change is more powerful than any anxiety people have about learning. Build that imperative into the training. Remind people why it's so important all the time. Get them to tell you why it's so critical.

Connect to people through their personal needs. For example, we were involved in a project with a travel organisation. The change agent saw that telephone sales reps were not benefiting from the new customer service system (the project was codenamed *"Mars"*). They were bored by the training and saw the new ways of operating as unduly complex and bureaucratic. The agent stopped the training roll-out and redesigned the workshop around *"How do you sell more using Mars?"* The new training galvanised the sales reps because the system was put into context for them and showed them ways to make more sales, and therefore more commission. This shift in training perspective really made them concentrate on the training. Five months after Mars was implemented, sales were up 12 per cent.

Learning can be a powerful way to engage people in the change. If the people who are to implement the change can see the benefits in action they are far more likely to maintain the change, especially if those benefits affect them personally. If, for example, someone uses a new IT system and realises that it saves them an hour every day or removes the need for a tedious task they don't enjoy, then they are going to keep on using the system and will probably encourage others to do the same.

Make the learning as easy as possible. You can do this by knowing that adults learn best by doing. Keep the inputs short and get people to practise on actual cases. Another feature of the *"Mars"* workshops mentioned above was that people practised on actual situations. You can also keep the learning in bite-sized pieces. Use cost-effective e-learning to teach people basic facts, but get them face to face to work on application, behaviour change and to remind them of the imperative.

Critically, allow sufficient time to learn and practise new skills before people are held accountable. People adopt new skills and behaviours in different ways and you have to give them enough time to integrate the new learning into their daily life. It's not realistic to expect someone to learn something on Monday and replicate it flawlessly by Friday. Our data shows that one of the easiest ways you can push people into resistance is by judging their performance too early. Give them time to assimilate what they have learned, otherwise it pushes all their anxiety buttons.

Learning can take many forms, so match the delivery to the people involved. You could use workshops, online training, coaching and well-structured on-the-job learning. For example, a large telecommunications client of ours was having trouble getting people to engage in their e-learning package. The problem was that their people spent so long sitting in front of computer screens that they didn't want to learn in that way as well. Moving the learning to a classroom environment was much more successful; they wanted to interact and talk with their colleagues. It was also a great way to engage people in the change. Learning can play a vital role in engaging people and helping them build commitment to the change.

Lastly, make the learning as practical as possible. People learn well when they can connect to what they know and can apply the learning right away. However, don't take this too far. According to the *Washington Post* a sales rep in Utah is suing his company after his boss waterboarded him as part of a team-building exercise. After the demonstration the boss reportedly said, *"You saw how hard Chad fought for air right there. I want you to go back inside and fight that hard to make sales."*

Rewards

Rewards are a real challenge for change agents. It can seem all so logical, but it is hard to do well. The data we collect from clients is very consistent on this point and states that rewarding people remains one of the highest risk factors in change.

The *"logic"* is that most change initiatives require extra effort from people. We have to establish new goals and find different ways of working and behaving. For example, you could reward behaviour change, milestone achievement, active involvement in the change and the willingness to test and pilot new approaches. Organisations should seek to reward the extra effort and any successful achievement of those goals. Conversely, we also need to send out a strong message that old ways of working and resisting change will not be rewarded.

The logic continues to say that rewards help to encourage people to change behaviour and reinforce new positive behaviours. In other words, rewards drive positive change or – at the very least – change will falter or fail if it is not aligned to the rewards people receive. Logic clearly assumes that if you can incentivise someone to change, they will change faster and better.

All of the above is *"generally"* correct. The only problem is that most change agents can do little to influence financial rewards within an organisation.

There are a number of reasons for this. In most organisations, the formal reward system is set annually. So if you are the change agent for a major cross-organisational project you might get that project incorporated into people's performance goals, which is likely to get their attention. But for most projects that is simply not possible. Additionally, it certainly appears hard to change compensation schemes for individuals or groups. Even if you can, compensation schemes of this nature are very hard to get right. Many times, the law of unintended consequences kicks in – where you want to get one result but inadvertently encourage another type of behaviour. And the last reason is that most companies are running multiple change programmes and it becomes next to impossible to align compensation plans with all of the activities.

But the good news is that you can encourage sponsors to give smaller rewards that are not tied to the company compensation system. Our work suggests that small rewards can have a disproportionate effect.

Four ways you can make rewards work

When discussing rewards it's easy to assume that the only reward worth having is financial. It's not. There are four other ways to use reward to facilitate and speed up change implementation success. Here they are:

1. Exceed people's expectations. Satisfaction is often the gap between what you receive and what you expected. In other words, satisfaction equals perception minus expectation. Small awards

can have a big impact on people's favourable view of the change. I remember being in a meeting with a European CIO and his team discussing rewards. Initially people were very sceptical about the whole topic but when they were asked to think again about what had worked for them in the past they began to list a host of things they believed had been effective. These ranged from letters from the CEO to project team members, impromptu celebrations, small financial awards such as gift tokens, thanks in public forums (*"it made me feel great"*) and small gifts sent to spouses or partners to recognise that project team members had been working sixteen-hour days. People in the team then talked about the positive effect these rewards had on them versus the possibility of a small incremental salary increase or even a bonus which could be tied to many factors. Pleasantly surprising people doesn't have to cost a fortune, but it can lubricate the change process enormously.

2. Give rewards as soon as possible after the result. Small rewards should be given very close to the event that warranted them – so if sponsors catch someone doing something successfully they should try to reward them within hours or days. This tends to be far more motivational than a delayed reward. Compare this with the annual bonus process where you can complete a project in February and get a reward the following January. No one even remembers what they are being rewarded for.

3. Make the rewards appropriate. Think about going around to a friend's for dinner. Your host cooks a great meal and at the end of the meal you hand over £30 and say, *"This is to thank you for a wonderful meal"*. Your host would probably be very offended. But if you took a £30 bottle of wine around it would be accepted gratefully and in the spirit it was intended. There is still something magical about receiving a handwritten thank-you card; perhaps it's because they are now so rare, what with email and text messaging. But that little extra effort can make the world of difference to people and make them feel good for days. The reason the card or bottle of wine is so effective is that they are a social gift and the £30 is a market price. They come with different expectations, implications and unspoken contracts. Given appropriately, small rewards can be much more powerful than money.

4. Make the rewards feel personal. This builds on the idea of appropriateness. I was at dinner with a change agent team once when they were about three-quarters of the way through a project and doing well. One of the main sponsors had arranged the dinner. Towards the end of the meal he gave a very short but thoughtful talk about how well they had done and then gave out, to each person, a small wrapped present. Inside was a pen with the name of the project inscribed on it. Everyone was delighted. But talking to the team the next day it was clear that while the pen was a nice gift what had really impressed them was the care the sponsor had taken with the present. To them it felt very personal. It wasn't something the organisation had given them but rather something their sponsor had given them. This made the reward much more motivational.

Communication

In our experience, people can get confused about the purpose of communication in change. The primary use of communication in change is to create clarity. You have to ensure that everyone at least understands what you are trying to achieve. Well-planned communication can also help people feel positive about a change and lessen the impact of resistance. The reverse is also true: poorly planned or executed communication will cause or heighten resistance.

The problem is that communication is often the only thing that leaders can think of when it comes to creating engagement. Poorly performing change agents are often far too fond of slides and emails which go unopened or are *"skim read"* at best. I have worked in the change arena for over 25 years and I have yet to meet a single person who has read an emailed presentation and been motivated to change by it. At best these are seen as a necessary evil. Their over-use springs from a mindset that if you put the case as logically as possible then people, being rational, will buy into it and take the appropriate set of actions. This type of *"communication"* is also used as a corporate *"get out of jail free"* card. Those involved with change can remain in their respective offices with their doors firmly closed, safe in the knowledge that when asked they can say, *"Well, it's not my fault; I told everyone what was going on"*. In fact, they didn't tell everyone – they sent them an email presentation. That is not communication; that is hiding behind technology.

A large number of organisations have become heavily reliant on written communication, something which goes directly against the human need for dialogue. We respond to two-way communication, so finding a way to open up conversation is a crucial step to powerful engagement processes.

Four ways you can communicate change effectively

Here are four ways you can be effective when communicating change.

1. Use face-to-face, two-way communication wherever possible. People value dialogue and conversation. It takes much longer than email but is infinitely more effective. Try and avoid going to all meetings with detailed and well-prepared presentations. They inhibit dialogue. Initiate a conversation with people. When I was working on the turnaround of an insurance company in California in the late 1980s we used an old concept called *"Brown Bag Lunches"*. Basically it meant that you could invite anyone you wanted from any level in the organisation to come and join you for a sandwich. You would talk for no more than five to ten minutes about the change, and then invite other people to talk, share ideas and raise objections. This approach was always so much more powerful than doing presentations. People felt they had a voice and an opportunity to express their views. It wasn't a panacea but it was certainly an early part of building acceptance for the change.

2. Enable your sponsors to demonstrate a real commitment to communication and be involved in the creation of the communication strategy. In my early years in change management I used to build change plans with my project team and then present them to the executive teams. I would get loads of head nodding and appropriate noises of support: *"We are right behind you."* And they were right behind me – miles behind me and I was out on my own. I soon realised that co-creation is critical to success. I thought I was helping by not involving them and just getting on with the plans, but it was a mistake and I still have the scar tissue to prove it. The more

executives take an active role in building the plan the more likely they are to take an active role in delivering it. And this doesn't have to be a long drawn out process; it can be done expertly and quickly.

3. Tailor messages to the receiver's perspective. We can often talk in a language no one further down the organisation understands, and people at different levels of an organisation can also see the issues differently. This can be because of different interests, history, culture or experiences. What people need and expect can also vary depending on their career stage: for example, those just out of college may need a different communication style to those nearing retirement. It is your job to speak to those differences. If you can connect to them you have an opportunity to get your message across.

4. Seek feedback and, where possible, take it on board. One of our clients had a global roll-out of a change a few years ago. It was cascaded through the regions to the different countries. Two weeks later an agency telephoned a sample of front-line workers in each country to ask them what they knew about the change. This survey provided a wealth of information on where countries had successfully communicated change. The countries that had not were then asked to redeliver the communication and were given coaching to help them be more effective.

Communication strategy and planning

There are four components to successful change communications:

- Brand
- Strategy
- Plan
- Measurement

Brand

Major change initiative communications often benefit from a distinctive brand. It can create an identity for the change and help create initial enthusiasm as it symbolises a break with the past. Some organisations avoid branding change as they want people to see change as being ongoing and part of everyday work. Plus, there is evidence to suggest that change brands contribute to employee cynicism about change. Nonetheless, most organisations will need to give change initiatives a name to make communication about the change easier. As such, practical concerns usually outweigh the negative aspects of branding a change initiative.

Strategy

A communication strategy outlines what is to be achieved through communication and the overall approach. Our experience is that executive involvement in planning communication strategies is critical to ensure leaders' commitment in delivering the necessary communication. A communication strategy would cover topics such as objectives, guiding principles, risk mitigation, key messages, style and tone. It sets the framework for the more detailed communication planning.

Plan

A communication plan details specific objectives and activities for the communication of a specific change initiative. It is guided by the communications strategy and is designed to build commitment for the change, reduce resistance and ensure implementation occurs. It would detail audience, methods of delivery, who, when and where. So the plan is much more specific, detailed and tactical than the strategy.

Measurement

Change communication tracks that the plan is becoming a reality. It allows change agents to appreciate the effect communication is having in terms of understanding, disposition and behaviour. It also allows you to take appropriate corrective or sustaining actions. Some time ago we worked with an organisation that used a form of telephone market research to find out what front-line workers had been told about a change. They found significant gaps in the basic understanding of the change between different geographical regions. This allowed the change agents to work with the underperforming regions to bring them up to the benchmark created by the best.

Key actions for building powerful engagement processes

Questions you need to answer in order to build powerful engagement processes include:

1. Can you use a variety of methods to engage people? You may need to use a mix of engagement methods to build commitment to your change initiative.

2. In addition to involvement, can you use learning, communications and rewards as ways to pull people into the change process? Having to issue instructions to people and hoping they will comply may result in change being accepted, but it rarely creates commitment.

3. Are you using different engagement approaches at different parts of the change? For example, rewards can be very wasteful if given too early in the change process; learning needs to be offered to people when they are ready to learn and can benefit from the investment.

4. Have you built a detailed engagement plan as part of your change planning? The devil is in the detail. For example, we see many involvement events fail because of inadequate planning and preparation. A rough rule of thumb is that it takes twice as long to properly plan an event as you think it will.

Powerful engagement processes allow people involved in change to become more committed to the change. This gives people confidence that the change is real and not just hot air, that the change is critical, and that they will be given enough time and the appropriate training to learn how to use the change successfully. This, coupled with rewards for working in the new way, soon emphasises that continuing to stick to the status quo is unacceptable. A powerful engagement process also gives people guidelines so they know exactly what is expected of them and how to focus their efforts for maximum success, which can help them to feel part of the change process and bring eventual success.

The first three critical success factors of change focused on how to create organisational change plans. Now it's time to cascade that change from organisation to local for full implementation success.

PART THREE:

Local success factors – helping people perform

8

Committed local sponsors – mobilising middle and front-line managers

When it comes to major change, there is something very pivotal about the role of middle and front-line managers – who we will call local sponsors for the rest of this chapter.

Figure 8.1: The Changefirst "Wheel": CSF 4 – Committed local sponsors

But it seems that in many organisations these managers have become disempowered and are seen as barriers to change rather than enablers. So many times I have sat in meetings and workshops and someone has drawn the diagram below.

Figure 8.2: Ineffective change

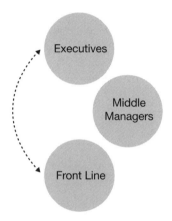

Basically, the story is always a variation on the following:

> **Executive:** *"These middle managers have blocked change in the past. So we are going to bypass them and go straight to the front-line associates."*
>
> **Me:** *"What will happen then?"*
>
> **Executive:** *"The front-line associates really want to change and they will put pressure on their managers to fall into line."*
>
> **Me (sceptically):** *"What's happened in the past when associates have put pressure on their managers to change?"*

I won't go on, but you get the picture. What this approach does is alienate local sponsors during change, leaving them unskilled and unmotivated to lead change effectively. I was with a senior executive of a company some years ago who described his middle management as *"permafrost"*. We were talking about how best to execute an important change throughout his organisation so that the change initiative was successfully implemented. This executive was adamant that cascading the change through middle management would be like hitting permafrost. For your information, and if like me you didn't know, permafrost covers a considerable area of the Arctic and measures up to four metres deep – so it's not that easy to get around or through. As such it was a fairly amusing but troublesome description of his middle management. He went on to say, *"It's a huge problem for us because every time we try and engage the 'permafrost' they resist and try to block the change."*

As a consequence of this *"permafrost"* – whether real or perceived – the company had defaulted to a change communication strategy that meant gathering everyone involved in the change from shop floor to management and announcing the change to them all at the same time. Needless to say, this strategy only served to entrench the permafrost by adding a few more layers.

This issue is extremely common and it's equally detrimental to the organisation and the chances of implementing change successfully. Instead of trying to involve local sponsors and getting them to support the change, or asking sponsors to help design the solution or to give feedback on implementation strategies, senior management bypass them. They announce the change to everyone at the same time and wonder why middle and first-line management resist change. This approach is your very own *"build your own permafrost"* kit.

Ineffective change always has some causes in common. One of these causes is when senior management decide the change is a *"secret"* so they don't share the initiatives with middle management. Instead they tell everyone from the shop floor to front-line and middle management all at the same time so it *"won't leak out"*. They then pull the managers aside after the event and tell them they have to help manage the change. Or, as one middle manager said to me, *"Yesterday I received an email announcing the change at the same time as the 20 people who work for me. At the bottom there was a note saying 'go see your manager if you need to know more'. It's like they are deliberately trying to undermine me."*

This approach does everything possible to make it as hard as possible for middle managers to buy into the change. They feel devalued and their credibility among their people drops. Plus, it takes a very special person not to say, *"What do you want me to say? I've just found out myself"* or *"There's no point asking me anything; I don't know any more than you do."*

You'd have to be a pretty exceptional leader to say something like, *"You know, I did hear about this when you did – but I was pretty sure it was going to happen and I've been thinking about it and I'm totally behind it. It's the right thing to do."* That would be quite a feat to pull off, especially when senior management have *"form"* in this area and have delivered news about major change in this way before.

The positive impact of local sponsors

On the other hand, we know that local sponsors can play a powerful role in change execution. They are in a unique place to push the change agenda. For example, they can help people see how the change is relevant to them, they can role model the change so that people can see what is expected of them and they can provide a *"buffer"* that can give people time to adjust. On top of that, they are often the most trusted by their people and so can be used as a sounding board to air concerns. They can help create a positive climate for change.

The two components of creating committed local sponsors are local role modelling, demonstrating the behaviours required for the change on a local level, and local manager's support, creating the conditions for their people to become committed.

Make local sponsors more effective

We need three steps to happen to make local sponsors effective. We need to work with organisational sponsors to build their commitment, we need to give them the change skills to be effective, and we need to help them sponsor change through role modelling the change and providing hands-on support for their people. Let's examine these steps one at a time.

Work with organisational sponsors to build their local commitment
Local sponsors can effectively block change by tactics such as ignoring the change, quietly expressing their resistance to other people, attempting to bargain away the change by saying they are too busy, or simply reinterpreting the change into something they want to happen. I witnessed this in 2003.

I was called up by a large global manufacturing company. Their CEO had taken personal responsibility for a change in operating procedures. The current operating procedures had failed to stop an accident that had caused quite a lot of damage to the surrounding environment: think BP in 2010 in Louisiana but on a much smaller scale. He was very upset about it and, after doing everything he could to put it right, he put a team together to rewrite the policy. He then decided he would implement the policy himself, so he travelled to each of the major plants and addressed the staff about the need for change and, in particular, about how important it was that the new procedures were followed.

Sometime later he learned that one of the plants had nearly caused a fatal accident. When the incident was audited he found out that the management had actually ignored the new procedures. He asked me if I would mind going to the plant and reporting back to him on why this might have happened. So one of our consultants went to the plant and interviewed all the key people apart from the plant manager, who had since left the company. The consultant came back, wrote a brief report and presented it to the CEO. The report was a few pages long and very simple in its conclusions. What had happened was that when the CEO had left the plant after his presentation, the plant manager had got the supervisors together and told them that the new operating procedures were not suitable for their plant. According to them, their country, culture and way of working were all different to what the CEO imagined. So, while the CEO was well intentioned, his plan would cause too much difficulty.

After the CEO cooled down we explored what had caused this. At the heart of the problem was the perception that the CEO had much less real power in the plant than the plant manager. The plant manager hired, promoted, fired and rewarded people; the CEO was a man who flew in from Europe and a person who even many of the supervisors wouldn't recognise. All he brought with him were words and slides, but no perceived power – so naturally they had followed the plant manager. This then got to the action. The CEO needed, first of all, to build the commitment of his plant managers to make the change work. He could only do this when he had got his direct reports to support the change. There is nothing very insightful here, but an understanding that to be successful you need to always treat local sponsors as people who need to build their own commitment first before you expect them to help others to commit and adapt.

Give local sponsors the change skills to be effective

It's very important that local sponsors can coach and help their people directly. If they don't have these skills then you should arrange training for them. Sponsor training usually falls into three categories and can be followed up by change agents coaching sponsors on the job. The three types of training include:

- Help with change leadership skills. How can sponsors lead change effectively?
- Assistance in how to help their people adapt to change. Sponsors need to learn how people adapt to change and the tactics they can use to help them
- Lastly, help with their own personal reactions to change. We call this *"putting your own oxygen mask on first"*. It's a bit like they tell you on a plane during the safety demonstration: when the oxygen masks come down, you need to help yourself first before assisting others. We believe it's crucial to help sponsors become more resilient. Less resilient managers will struggle to help their own people during times of uncertainty

Help them sponsor change through role modelling the change and providing hands-on support for their people

If a change involves using a new customer relationship management system and the local sponsor still uses the old system, he or she can't really be surprised if the other users continue with the old system too. Even if the local sponsor then reprimands them for this behaviour, the users will not change unless they can see their leader role modelling the change that he or she wishes them to make.

Role modelling change is a basic staple of conventional change management theory. After all, it's common sense – you can't honestly expect others to do what you will not do yourself. There are, however, challenges associated with role modelling the change.

The first is the sponsor's lack of self-awareness. In these cases, sponsors will think they are modelling the change when they are not. In a recent discussion a client told me that they were involving their people because the change was to create a leaner but more team-based, knowledge-based organisation. People would need to work more autonomously and collaboratively. He said that he was *"walking the talk"* by being more involving, more consultative. I discovered, fairly quickly, that he had only done this with a small group of about 15 senior specialists and not the whole team. The rest of the team, some 150 people, had received what appeared to be a normal set of written communications about the change. In other words, they were told to change. I tried to help him see what had happened through the eyes of the 150, not the 15. He began to see how his *"role modelling"* could be sending out contradictory messages.

The second issue we see time and again is that sponsors don't know how they can role model a change. A few years ago I was talking about the need for role modelling with a group of executives in a South African company that was implementing SAP. They all nodded sagely and in apparent agreement – until one brave soul eventually said that he had no idea how exactly he could role model the behaviours he needed for SAP to be implemented. He saw the importance of doing so but had no idea of how to go about it. So we began to brainstorm all the possibilities. Two hours later we had a list of five actions they could take so staff would actually see their commitment to SAP. You, as a change agent, need to help sponsors with this transition.

One of the fundamental roles of the local sponsor is to personally create the conditions for people to embrace the change and become committed to successful implementation. The job of the local sponsor is to work out how to get people to commit to the change and to change their behaviours. So, for example, a change agent was helping with a technology company who were rolling out a new manufacturing process. She designed a series of workshops to run in each plant to help the plant managers build the implementation plan. The plant managers had to run those workshops in their own locations, so it was imperative that they were on board. To facilitate that process all the plant managers were first brought to a central location and more senior sponsors were on hand to build their commitment to the change. The change agent also gave them some of the PCI tools to help them go back and sustain the change. This process made them feel valued and they felt able to go back and cascade the change through their local area.

Key actions for creating committed local sponsors

The questions you need to answer to create local sponsors include these:

1. Have you engaged local sponsors in the change before announcing the change to the rest of the staff? Can you involve them in designing the change and planning implementation?

2. Have you checked how committed they are before you cascade the change any further? Do they need more coaching and support?

3. Have you closed any skill gaps that sponsors may have in terms of helping their people adapt to change? Increasing local sponsor capacity to effectively handle change will pay huge dividends in the long run.

4. Can you engage local sponsors in building an implementation plan for their area?

What support can you offer local sponsors as they work with their people to build their commitment and help them to adapt? Be very careful not to step in and assume the sponsor's role if they are not supporting the change. It may be very tempting, but you rarely have enough power to be successful. Taking over their role is usually a strong predictor of change installation or failure.

When you have taken the time to create committed local sponsors those affected by the change are able to connect to it. Often change projects initiated at the organisational level can be abstract and distant. Having local sponsors translate the change into meaningful language and show people how it is relevant to their daily working lives at a local level is fundamental to success.

Committed local sponsors are also on hand to disseminate essential change information before rumour and misinformation has a chance to derail the process, and they can also reiterate the imperative for change should it all seem a little too hard and the comfort of the old way seem tempting. These individuals act as a helpful buffer between those on the ground making the change happen, working with the change on a daily basis, and organisational HQ – so they often act as an invaluable sounding board and agony aunt all rolled into one. People feel much safer sounding off to a committed local sponsor than they do to head office, and as such are much more likely to air grievances before hostility and resentment stalls the process. In this supportive and less formal environment they are also much more likely to offer potential solutions which could then build commitment to the change, especially if those suggestions are taken on board or at least followed up. And, finally, committed local sponsors can personalise the change for individuals on the ground so they can see how the change will benefit them. All of which helps as a launch pad for creating the next critical success factor for change – strong personal connections.

9

Strong personal connection – building personal commitment to change

I once had an interesting experience that explains the difficulty of building personal commitment to change. I was talking to a potential client about their change implementation track record. The executive from this organisation told me that their track record was mixed but they were particularly proud of a new sales-tracking tool that had been implemented the year before. He told me that the tool had gone live in record time. Not only that, but people seemed to like it and, more importantly, it was enabling more effective ways of managing sales across multiple geographies and also enabling a more customer-centred way of doing business.

The interesting part of this is that a good friend of mine is one of the company's best business development professionals. So the next time I had a drink with him I asked him what he thought of the new sales tool. He told me that it wasn't a *"bad tool"* but in reality he did the minimum to comply with the requirements of the system. He found it intrusive and struggled to see how it improved his personal sales performance (and thus increased his sales incentive, of course). So he accepted that the change might be necessary *"for other people"*, but wasn't personally committed to it.

This story articulates the challenge of building personal commitment. How do we translate the needs of the organisation into something that

Figure 9.1: The Changefirst "Wheel": CSF 5 – Strong personal connection

people can buy into? Our data suggests that only about 30 per cent of people actually become committed to a single change. When we reviewed the data we also found that those people who said they were committed rated their organisations far higher on helping them to personally connect to the change and adapt to the new way of working. Helping people to personally connect to the change is clearly very important.

There are three positive outcomes of doing so:

1. You achieve longer-term change in behaviour sooner by making people feel more informed, valued and involved.

2. You build higher levels of personal control. If people feel a personal connection to the change they are able to regain a sense of control more quickly.

3. Finally, you give answers to people's most basic questions about any change: how is this going to affect me, what do you want me to do and what's in it for me?

And there are three components of a strong personal connection:

1. **Personal imperative** – people realising that they personally need to change.
2. **Solution viability** – people believing the changes they have to make are achievable.
3. **Being successful** – people understanding how they can be successful.

Principles for building commitment

In a moment I will review how you can build commitment. But before then I want to review three general principles about building commitment in people during major change.

Principle one is that this is work best done by the local sponsors. They are the sponsors who can connect to the people who need to change; we covered this in the previous chapter. You need to train them, coach them and reward them to do this work. If they can't or won't do it, you need to build a commitment plan for them first. Be very, very careful of working with uncommitted sponsors.

Principle two is that you need to ask people. This sounds like simple common sense, but often it's not common practice. Consulting firms make millions of pounds from doing just that. You tell them you have a problem with a change. They say they can fix it. What they do is go and ask the people affected what the problem is and, sometimes, what they would do to fix it. The consultant then uses that information to tell you what you need to do to fix the problem. As Robert C. Townsend, a former chairman and president of Avis Rent-a-Car who went on to write the bestselling book *Up the Organization: How to Stop the Corporation from Stifling People and Strangling Profits* famously said: *"Consultants are people who borrow your watch and tell you what time it is, and then walk off with the watch."* But, you know, they are doing the work in the only way that's possible: you have to ask the people what the issue is and, ideally, how they would fix it. There is no other way to find out – other than by guessing, which is not a great management tool. We constantly advocate asking through the use of our survey tools, focus groups and interviews.

The third principle links to the second, and that is that you have to start where people are, not where you want them to be. It can sound *"soft"* but it's important work. People observe the world through what are called *"frames of reference"* – a set of ideas they hold through which other ideas are interpreted or assigned meaning. People use their personal frame of reference to gather information, make judgements and determine how to get things done. For example, they may view the issues causing the change in a different way to you. They may not even accept there is a need for the change in the first place, or they may have very different expectations or success criteria than you do. You need to learn to understand the change through their eyes and base your change tactics on how they see the world and not how you see it, otherwise you are always talking to people at cross purposes. Ultimately you want people to see the world through your frame of reference, but the paradox is that you can only do so by starting with theirs. In a recent change we saw this play out. It wasn't until the sponsor was able to find out what the frames of reference were that she could begin to deal with people's negative reactions to the change. In the end she was able to shift the frame of reference for most of the people by a mixture of involvement and persuasion. For the rest, she was left with some tough decisions. Their ideas were too deeply held, the cost of giving them up was too high or they simply lacked the adaptability to be able to change themselves.

How people build commitment

The commitment curve describes the stages people go through to become committed to a change. Your job is to help sponsors move their people sequentially through each stage. At any point on the curve, up to the last one, people can still resist the change. People might move up one stage, then hit a barrier and begin to resist the change. It's important to then go back and build the actions necessary to get that person back on board and moving up the commitment curve again - see Figure 9.2.

Part of your change plan needs to include action steps that you can use at each stage of the change process. Use local change agents to provide intelligence on how people are feeling and their views and perspectives on the change. Do what you can to take those opinions into account, and make sure that people know when you have.

The commitment curve relates to the stages from Awareness to Commitment that people go through in change. Those stages are:

- Hear
- Understand
- Support
- Act
- Use
- Own

Each stage on the commitment curve offers you opportunities for building commitment.

- **Hear:** this step is where you connect the shared change purpose to people's everyday work. Spend time on sharing information about the change with people. It would be great if people were positive, but it's not essential. Focus on helping people think through the implications for them. This would be the time when you could begin to help people understand why the current state has to change. Think carefully about timing. Some organisations can leave this too late, which means that by the time they tell people their network has beaten them to it – and in our experience networks rarely put a positive spin on change. It's better to tell people about change too early than too late

- **Understand:** those affected by change will move up the commitment curve to understanding when they have the opportunity to discuss

Figure 9.2: The commitment curve

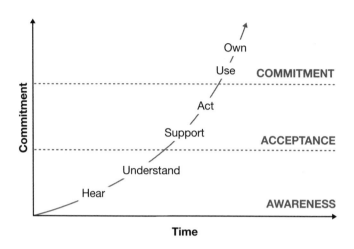

the issues connected to the change. So, for instance, you could create local examples that will enable individuals to see how their contributions will be essential for the change. This is a good time to get feedback from people about their literal understanding of the change. By getting people to repeat back to you their understanding of the change you can better appreciate what messages are getting through and what messages are getting confused. This is a great opportunity to make sure that what the company wants and what people assume it wants are the same thing

- **Support:** people will support the change when they can begin to see how the change will benefit them in some way and believe it is possible for them to be successful in the new way of working. So, for example, you could help them explore the details of the change initiative and give them the opportunity to ask questions, or you could ask them to participate in teams to work on specific aspects of the change. Remember to reward early adopters as they can be positive role models for others

- **Act:** testing is an incredibly important stage. Just as consumers are usually unwilling to buy products they cannot test, so people are often unwilling to commit to change without first trying it out. So, for example, you could create temporary systems that allow people to practise before the change has been fully implemented or you could let people visit other parts of the organisation that have successfully adopted the change

- **Use:** this is the first level of commitment and it means exactly that. People are asked to start using the change in their daily work. It's at this point that change needs reinforcing and tracking. So, for example, you could track how many people are using the change or you could recognise *"early wins"* where people have successfully used the new way of working. You need to make a conscious decision about what level of commitment you need for specific parts of the business. It will determine your commitment-building strategies

- **Own:** the final level of commitment to the change. This is a point where reinforcement is necessary. So, for example, you could ensure sponsors continue to role model behaviours or you could deal with any lingering issues that may impede personal performance. There are also opportunities to enlist people in continuous improvement of the change

Key actions for making strong personal connection

The questions you need to answer to help others to make strong personal connections to the change include:

1. Do you really understand the impact of the change on people who will have to change? Do you understand the change from their perspective?

2. Are you clear about what people will need to do to be successful? Have you helped them learn and practise the new way of working so they can picture success?

3. Have you prepared local sponsors so they can help their people build commitment in their own people?

4. Have you built your engagement plans (involvement, learning, rewards and communications) from the perspective of those who will need to change or from the organisational perspective? It's the former that drives success.

5. Do you have a way to assess progress towards commitment? We have a tool called Initiative Risk Assessment that tells you the level of people's commitment and why they are where they are; you can find out more information on this and other PCI tools from www.changefirst.com/change. There are also other ways to achieve this, such as focus groups and interviews.

As a change agent, if you foster strong personal connections to the change then those people affected by the change will commit to it sooner and without as much resistance. When people affected by change are able to appreciate how the change will benefit them personally in some way, or at the very least will not make their life harder, they are much more likely to get on board. Once people are on board you will reduce the impact of change, shorten the transition period and get people back to full productivity in as short a time as possible.

When people can see the personal ramifications of change and of not changing, they are usually more willing to change because they will regain that much-needed sense of control over their environment. As such you will achieve long-term behavioural change sooner because people feel informed and valued, and that their role and they themselves have all been considered in the change. Even when that is not actually true, there are always ways to personalise the change, and this personalisation allows those affected to gain confidence, raise concerns and have them appropriately addressed. You may even receive some really useful insights that could improve the change and make it easier and faster to implement. All that is left now is to sustain personal performance and embed the change into normal working life.

10

Sustaining personal performance – helping people adapt to change

I can remember the first time I faced serious resistance. I was a young and naive manager. My boss had asked me to build and launch a performance tool for the IT group. This naivety came about when I tried to put a team together to co-build the tool and was told, *"we're too busy"*. Rather than failing on the project I went ahead without help and built, if I may say so, an excellent tool. For the time, it was a real *"state of the art"* application. I actually thought I had done extremely well to build it. It looked beautiful and practical. Remember pride always comes before a fall.

When I presented it to the IT senior team their reactions were logical, emotional, candid and, above all, negative. And most of it was really about me: my lack of consultation, my lack of understanding about their jobs, my rush to complete this without talking to them. I had experienced real *"resistance"* for the first time.

At a societal level we saw the same reactions in Europe in 2010 after proposed welfare cuts, pay freezes, increased taxes, demands to retire later on less, and so on. When this sort of action happens you can really see how universal the commonalities of change are across organisations, communities and countries. You can see how people react when

Figure 10.1: The Changefirst "Wheel": CSF 6 – Sustaining personal
performance

well-established norms and conventions are challenged and changed.
People's loss of control is obvious. You see denial *("our country can pay off
its debts without cutting public expenditure")* turn rapidly to shock *("how
could they!")* and convert into anger *("politicians are terrible people")*.
Lastly, a few people are already moving into the bargaining stage *("we'll
keep working hard if you give us a salary increase this year")*.

On the other side of the change curve, there are people in business
who have adapted to the new situation: continuing recession. They had,
after all, been working on this since 2008. People began to talk about
"the new reality", *"living in a new paradigm"*, *"what we have learned"*
and saying things like *"this is not temporary, so we need to continuously
adjust"*. Many of these people have reached acceptance of the change,
but it may have taken them two years to get there. Interestingly, my
observation would be that many got to logical acceptance first but it then
took their emotions about six months to catch up.

This chapter is all about how to manage people's reactions to change and the things you need to do to help people adapt to it. Sustained personal performance happens when personal concerns and reactions are being effectively addressed.

The underlying hypothesis is that during major change people's performance drops. Their productivity and work quality is likely to drop because they are going through the various stages of change. They are adapting, or attempting to adapt, to the change they perceive is happening. It is important, therefore, that front-line managers and local agents have the skills to help the people affected by change to navigate it. It is certainly important that you are able to train and coach local sponsors to help their people.

Personal reactions to change are incredibly important. Change management is often described as a *"contact sport"*: how true. Sponsors need to work closely with people to use discussion, coaching and involvement as ways to help them adapt. J.P. Garnier, as mentioned in Chapter Two, said, *"Getting people to change – one by one – is the only way to change organisations. After all, every change is personal."* Change succeeds one person at a time and it fails in exactly the same way. Personal concerns need addressing. People might think the change is a good idea, but if they are hitting issues like potential financial insecurity or worsening work relationships they may well decide the cost of the change exceeds the benefits they will gain from it. Unless you address personal concerns you will never fully implement the change.

Poor management of people's reactions to change can also have long-term negative impacts on the organisation. Organisations can believe that *"people will get over it"*. In other words, you can make people comply and think that they will eventually forget this and move on. They don't. I remember when I was working in California for American Express and made two IT people redundant. They were not thrilled about it but neither were they upset; it was the early 1990s in California, IT jobs were plentiful and they were given a good redundancy package. One of them came into my office later in the day and asked if she could just leave without working her notice so she could get on with finding another job. I agreed and asked if she would like a hand getting her stuff out. She was grateful. I called a security guard as it was late evening, and he came and helped her get her belongings to her car. Next morning I walked in and there were a lot of very hostile people glaring at me. I asked my assistant what had happened and she told me that it was because I had *"got someone marched off the premises"* the previous night. I got them all together to tell them what had happened but it turned out it was far worse than I thought. Ten years ago the organisation had been owned by another business. One day they got everyone together and announced redundancies amounting to about 25 per cent of the workforce. The way they did it was to tell everyone to go back to their desk. If there was a box with an envelope on the desk that meant they needed to pack up and security guards would be around within the hour to escort them out of the building. A decade later there were still a few survivors from that incident who felt it was happening all over again. They clearly hadn't *"got over it"*.

The key components of sustained personal performance are:

- **Future security** – people need to believe that their job security will be the same or enhanced as a result of the change
- **Financial impact** – people need to believe that their earnings or salary will be the same or increased as a result of the change
- **Work relationships** – people need to believe that their relationship with colleagues will be the same or improved as a result of the change
- **Level of responsibility** – people need to believe that their level of job responsibility will be the same or improved as a result of the change
- **Learning curve** – people need to believe that their personal performance will only be judged after they have had sufficient time to practise performing in the new way

Principles for helping people adapt to change

Remember in previous chapters we discussed how helping people adapt is work best done by the local sponsors. You need to ask people, involve people and you have to start the communication from where people are, not where you want them to be. These things still apply, but when seeking to sustain personal performance there are three additional principles to consider.

1. Principle one is to treat resistance as a natural by-product of organisational change. People can be logical, emotional, uncertain, controlling, kind and adversarial all in the space of five minutes. Employees are usually signed-up members of the human race; in other words, they will act as people tend to act. Many sponsors still believe that if they just make a compelling enough case for change then somehow all the annoying human-nature stuff will get circumvented or neutralised. Unfortunately it rarely works like that. Even if people are positive when they hear the case for change, it's entirely possible that they will still resist. So expect it and deal with it when you see it.

2. Principle two is that human reactions to change are normal, so help people understand their own reactions to change. One of the most powerful tools you can share with people is the Kübler-Ross Curve mentioned in Chapter Two. Many people will have seen the Kübler-Ross model which details the progression someone takes through grief. Kübler-Ross identified five stages of transition for patients facing death. This model was later adopted by organisational psychologists as a way of describing how people reacted to change. It's fair to say that the model has its critics, but it is still a reliable model to use and frankly I've not seen a better one. For those in the throes of change, knowing that their reactions are *"normal"* and that everyone on the planet goes through the same stages when dealing with change can be very comforting. Knowing there is a well-trodden path to travel helps people identify where they currently are and what they can do to help themselves. Plus, it reassures them that there is an end in sight which makes

it less likely for them to bounce out the change and retreat to their current state.

3. Principle three is that you should expect people to go backwards as well as forwards. Change and the stages of change are not linear. People don't neatly trot through the stages to acceptance. Often they might arrive at acceptance and fall back to anger; they may move forward and then appear to lose their way and regress to denial. This is just part of being human and is no cause for alarm. Helping people to understand that can make a huge positive difference to the speed and success of change, not to mention the stress levels normally associated with change.

Prochaska, Norcross and Diclemente, in their book *Change for Good*, refer to this process as the *"spiral model"* of change. They suggest that relapses are the rule rather than the exception when it comes to change. Those affected by change can often feel as though they have failed and that all their efforts have been in vain. Yet this is not the case. Change involves a forward and backwards process that eventually leads to success. Knowing that this is common and can be cured simply by moving forward can really help those affected deal with change.

Stages of change

We have indentified eight possible stages of change:

- **Early interest:** sometimes change gets off to a good start. At the early interest stage people are often overly enthusiastic. They don't really know what the change will entail and this *"uninformed optimism"* can lead to a tendency to ignore or dismiss possible downsides to the change. You need to praise the early support. At the same time, keep communication focused on the need for more understanding so that together you can set realistic expectations.

This stage was not in Kübler-Ross's model, but we have included it in our organisational model because this is what we observe - see Figure 10.2 on page 127. Often it occurs before people really know the true impact the change will have on them personally. Obviously this early shock does not occur in situations when the impact is clear, such as when personal adversity strikes – for example, being made redundant.

- **Shock:** this stage is well described by Kübler-Ross. When someone is told bad news, for example, it is not unusual for them to become very quiet or even to appear as though the news hasn't registered or affected them in any way. Those affected by change often feel that they can't relate to the change and don't understand where they fit in, so they often feel unable to discuss it with anyone.

In this stage you need to focus on building and maintaining positive relationships, especially in less formal environments. Everyone is different, so it's best to allow space and time for people to work through their own thinking at their own pace. Make sure they know there is a sounding board available if they need one.

- **Denial:** performance can continue to drop as those affected by change move into denial. Here those affected by change will simply ignore information, meetings and deadlines. No information is sought out and they will continue to plan using the old ways.

It's never wise to make overzealous challenges or confront people in the denial stage. Instead just encourage them to take small steps towards the change, such as reading some material or attending a meeting. Set simple and short-term change-related tasks and follow up afterwards. The follow up should be face to face and one on one, but informal. Encourage people to share their experience.

- **Anger:** needless to say, performance isn't optimal at the anger stage, but it's just part of the process. Typically those at this stage will be frustrated; they will have knee-jerk reactions to information which can occasionally be accompanied by emotional outbursts.

This is all normal behaviour as people feel anxious about the change and are unsure of their ability to adapt. Often this is based on fear and

Figure 10.2: Stages of change

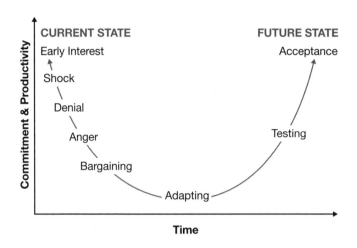

can lead to backstabbing, frosty silences and grudged compliance. In effect, people do the bare minimum and not a scrap more. Your best support tactic to help people through this stage is acceptance: accept signs of anger as legitimate and don't trivialise them. Listen to people without necessarily offering solutions. Don't be pushed into making snap decisions or trying to find a solution that perhaps doesn't yet exist.

Let people know you understand their frustration, and don't take it personally when someone gets angry with you. Remember, when people are expressing feelings of loss always accept them, don't rationalise or trivialise them.

- **Bargaining:** at the bargaining stage, which is still not very productive, people will try to negotiate compliance in return for other benefits. You might hear statements such as, *"Well, OK, I'll do it – but only if you can get X to do Y."* You will also hear excuses for why things have not been done. Those people who are stuck in the bargaining stage will often use workload and prioritisation to avoid the change, and request extensions or additional resources as a result. You need to recognise that the person is moving towards change and acknowledge their effort.

Encourage them to appreciate that everyone is in the same boat and that perfect performance is not expected. Be very careful about allowing concessions and be sure you fully understand the implications. Deal with all attempts at bargaining one to one, not in groups. Remember that all the stages up to this one are attempts by the people affected to return to the status quo.

- **Adapting:** those who are adapting have hit the bottom of the change curve. They have stuck with the change and are beginning to regain some control. It is the loss of control that people affected by change feel the most. The stability of the known current state is comfortable, and when that stability is challenged people affected by change can feel anxious and their performance inevitably drops. You should recognise that this is a pivotal moment in change, and everyone who reaches this stage should be rewarded and encouraged. Intrinsic rewards such as praise and recognition for effort can go a long way in moving those people back up the positive side of the change and productivity curve. You need to give people time to adapt. Try and persuade sponsors not to act too hastily.

- **Testing:** when those affected by change enter the testing stage they will set trial time deadlines. They will be willing to evaluate the impact of the change and will set about debugging the early challenges, thus improving the change. These behaviours demonstrate acceptance and indicate that the person concerned appreciates their long-term future associated with the change. You need to continue to encourage those willing to act, especially the early pioneers.

Review people's learning and seek opinion and feedback for improvement. Extend the level of involvement and ownership of decision making to those who are testing the change and adding value.

- **Accepting:** when people are truly in the acceptance stage they will have fixed any early change bugs. They will be as productive as they were prior to the change and will be comfortable using the change. They will be interested in continuous improvement of the change, especially if the change has benefited them personally in some way. As a change agent this is your goal – to get as many people as possible to this stage and beyond. When people affected by change accept and embrace the change, acknowledge them publicly and privately for their efforts. Involve people in identifying key lessons learned to improve future change capability. Use appropriate rewards and initiate continuous improvement efforts to maintain momentum.

Sustained personal commitment is the other side of the coin from strong personal connection. The latter is about how to build commitment in others, and sustained personal performance is about acknowledging that change affects people and people are not linear or logical. They can charge ahead one minute and resist the next, and being able to support people through that process is an essential part of implementing and sustaining successful change.

How quickly people cycle through these phases and how long they stay in each one depends on the individual and your ability to manage reactions and assist them to move through the change process.

Key actions for sustaining personal performance

The questions you need to answer to help others to sustain personal performance include these:

1. Have you identified groups critical to the change and created a plan for that group? Some groups may have more leverage over the success of the change than others. How can you maximise the change effort there?

2. Do key people have a transition plan that helps them change? People can need quite detailed help when they transition. Organisations often have an organisational plan, but not a personal change plan for individuals.

3. Are you looking out for resistance and where necessary encouraging it to surface? The most dangerous challenge often comes when

resistance goes underground: *"When someone is negative, if you listen carefully you can hear what's really going on. If you can find out why there is resistance, you can learn a lot about your project and about your chances for success. You may even end up with a better project."* That's Charles Fishman, in his April 1997 Fast Company article, *Change: Few can do it. Few can sustain it. Few can survive it.*

4. Can you track where people are on the reactions to change curve? If you know where people are, you can help them to appreciate that their feelings are a normal part of change and move through the process into acceptance. Look for ways to move them on to the next stage wherever you can.

As a change agent, your ultimate goal is Implemented change and sustained personal performance. Creating a shared change purpose lets everyone know where you are going; effective change leadership provides the compass for key people committed to the goal. Powerful engagement processes provide the maps so you can effectively avoid the ravines, find the safe havens and uncover the shortcuts. Engaged and committed local sponsors act as the indigenous trackers who are able to shorten the journey still further through useful local knowledge. These trackers help to ensure that everyone in the party knows why they are taking the journey in the first place, and paint a picture that inspires and motivates everyone involved so they can overcome the inevitable hardships along the way.

Arriving safely is then only a matter of time. Having worked through the highs and lows of the change process it would be extremely frustrating, therefore, to see all the good work fall away. Sustained personal performance is therefore all about embedding that change so that the new way is part of everyday life, and those involved in the change feel the effort was worth it, and the organisation can reap the rewards promised by the change. Sustaining personal performance therefore generates real ownership of the change and prevents personal concerns inhibiting change acceptance.

132 successfulCHANGE

Conclusion

Conclusion

I wanted to leave you with three of my personal learnings about being an agent of change. I have called the headings preparation, practice and preservation, and I've tried to finish by getting you to think about what you need to be effective. By effective I don't just mean successfully implementing change – although that is important – but how you can both enjoy and learn from all the change you are involved with. If you can master the process introduced to you in this book then your chances of implementing change successfully are greatly increased. You will never be fazed by change again, and the confidence you will feel in the face of change will make the whole process much more enjoyable and an opportunity to showcase your change management skills.

Learning One: Preparation

Most people start to realise that they don't know enough about change management when they are about a quarter of the way through their first change implementation. I tried to describe this earlier and showed how it happened to me. If you want to avoid my error (and terror!), then I strongly advise that you become a student of change now, before you are called to implement it. Avoid the fad-surfing stuff that pervades much of what passes for change management and look at the material and thoughts that have stood the test of time, certainly for the last 30 to 40 years and maybe the last millennium. Get yourself a set of tools, processes and training that will give you a head start. We at Changefirst would like that to be our training and certification because we believe it is the best, and countless happy clients agree. But whatever you decide, get yourself the right tools and training – before you need it! Developing change management skills will never be a wasted effort. Change is a constant part of almost any role in any business. Those who are proficient and effective in implementing successful change will be the leaders and executives of tomorrow.

Learning Two: Practice

I have come back to the idea of practice being central to learning recently. Dr. K. Anders Ericsson, a psychologist, is widely credited with being the person who came up with the idea that it takes 10,000 hours to master something. These thoughts have been incorporated in books such as Malcolm Gladwell's *Outliers* and Matthew Syed's *Bounce*. In certain talent management work the concept is called *"domain expertise"*. It all comes down to the reality that you need to practise something to get really good at it. We have a great group of change consultants who run workshops around the world for us. Most of them are former change managers who learned facilitation skills after thousands of hours of being change managers. They then joined Changefirst and now facilitate workshops at least six days a month. This adds up to a minimum of 500 hours of facilitation time a year, and you get really good at something when you do it that often. So they started with maybe 5000 hours of practice, and every year they add to that another 500 hours. To be an expert you have to practise regularly, and do so with focused feedback. The point is that if you want to get really good at change and make yourself professionally indispensable you need to take change seriously and practise your craft. Start the journey, get yourself assigned to projects, try new techniques, fail and pick yourself up again. Volunteer for training courses and keep learning. The minute you say you know everything you need to know about change is the day you lose your edge.

Learning Three: Preservation

On one of our workshops we use a phrase called *"put your own mask on first"* – we looked at it earlier. It's based on the safety procedure on a plane. The instructions tell you that if you try and help someone else before you help yourself you could pass out, thereby killing both of you. I think there's a lot to be said for that in a change agent's life. You can be under enormous stress trying to deliver projects on time and if you are not careful you will ultimately suffer. I've even witnessed a change agent who literally had a nervous breakdown in front of me. Don't ever let that happen to you. Think about these points:

- How can you preserve or increase your own levels of energy around change? This is often called resilience, defined as the ability to bounce back from adversity. How can you preserve this valuable personal resource?

- How do you *"rest"* between projects? Going from one project to another without a break can be a major stressor. Find ways to take time out. We often find in organisations that certain people always get selected for these change roles. The organisation becomes dependent on them. The problem is that if you are one of these people you can find yourself moving from one major change to another without respite.

- How can you make sure you are only responsible for what you can control? The danger in major change projects is that you take the responsibility for everything only to crumble under the weight.

My final advice would be not to engage in every change that comes along. Being good at change management is not about being a change junkie. It's about selecting the changes where you can really make a difference. Don't get addicted to the buzz. Rather listen to the words of an unknown soldier supposedly found in 1945:

"We trained hard, but it seemed that every time we were beginning to form up into teams, we would be reorganised. I was to learn later in life

that we tend to meet any new situation by reorganising; and a wonderful method it can be for creating the illusion of progress while producing confusion, inefficiency and demoralisation."

Changefirst have been dedicated to the understanding of successful change for over 25 years. In our research, and in working with leaders in organisations undergoing major change, we have been in the unique position to distil the dynamics of successful change. Our role has been to transfer that recipe to others so that they can develop change capabilities in their own organisations and move confidently into the future, safe in the knowledge that when change is necessary they have the internal skills to pull it off.

Truth is, change is often a messy business. As Charles Fishman so eloquently put it in the *Fast Company* article mentioned in Chapter Ten:

"If you read the academic literature, too often change comes across as a remarkably bloodless activity: establish a vision, find a mentor, design the program, paint by the numbers. We interrupt this program to deliver a dose of reality: it doesn't work that way. In the real world of change, leaders desert you, your staunchest allies cut and run, opposition comes from the places you least expect, and your fiercest opponent can turn out to be your most vital supporter. In other words, when emotions are running high and the stakes are even higher, people act like people."

If change was a simple process then every company would be successfully implementing change left, right and centre, but they are not. Year in, year out, companies all over the world are wasting millions (probably billions) on failed, forgotten or half-baked change. Those who can successfully implement worthwhile benefit-driven change are in the minority – so logical, rational solutions clearly don't hold the key. The reason for that is because people are what make change successful and people are often neither logical nor rational. It follows, therefore, that if you want a formula for consistent change implementation and delivery you have to focus on the people – and that's exactly what people-centred implementation is all about.

Index